teach
yourself

instant greek
elisabeth smith
language consultant:
dennis couniacis

For UK orders: please contact Bookpoint Ltd, 130 Milton Park, Abingdon, Oxon OX14 4SB. Telephone: +44 (0) 1235 827720. Fax: +44 (0) 1235 400454. Lines are open from 09.00–18.00, Monday to Saturday, with a 24-hour message answering service. Details about our titles and how to order are available at www.teachyourself.co.uk

For USA order enquiries: please contact McGraw-Hill Customer Services, PO Box 545, Blacklick, OH 43004-0545, USA. Telephone: 1-800-722-4726. Fax: 1-614-755-5645.

For Canada order enquiries: please contact McGraw-Hill Ryerson Ltd., 300 Water St, Whitby, Ontario L1N 9B6, Canada. Telephone: 905 430 5000. Fax: 905 430 5020.

Long renowned as the authoritative source for self-guided learning – with more than 30 million copies sold worldwide – the *Teach Yourself* series includes over 300 titles in the fields of languages, crafts, hobbies, business, computing and education.

British Library Cataloguing in Publication Data: a catalogue record for this title is available from the British Library.

Library of Congress Catalog Card Number: On file

First published in UK 2000 by Hodder Headline Ltd., 338 Euston Road, London NW1 3BH

First published in US 2000 by Contemporary Books, A Division of the McGraw Hill Companies, 1 Prudential Plaza, 130 East Randolph Street, Chicago, Illinois 60601 USA.

This edition published 2003.

Typeset by Transet Limited, Coventry, England.
Printed in Great Britain for Hodder & Stoughton Educational, a division of Hodder Headline Ltd., 338 Euston Road, London NW1 3BH by Cox & Wyman Ltd., Reading, Berkshire.

Papers used in this book are natural, renewable and recyclable products. They are made from wood grown in sustainable forests. The logging and manufacturing processes conform to the environmental regulations of the country of origin.

Impression number   10 9 8 7 6 5 4
Year   2007 2006 2005 2004

contents

If, like me, you usually skip introductions, don't! Read on! You need to know how **Instant Greek** works and why.

When I decided to write the **Instant** series I first called it *Barebones*, because that's what you want: *no frills, no fuss, just the bare bones and go!* So in **Instant Greek** you'll find:

- Less than 500 words to say everything, well ... nearly everything.

- No ghastly grammar – just a few useful tips.

- No time wasters such as ... 'the pen of my aunt...'

- No phrase book phrases for a working breakfast with the offspring of Onassis.

- No need to struggle with the Greek script – everything is in easy phonetic language.

- No need to be perfect. Mistakes won't spoil your success.

I have put some 30 years of teaching experience into this course. I know how people learn. I also know for how long they are motivated by a new project (a few weeks) and how little time they can spare to study each day (under an hour). That's why you'll complete **Instant Greek** in six weeks and get away with 45 minutes a day.

Of course there is some learning to do, but I have tried to make it as much fun as possible, even the boring bits. You'll meet Tom and Kate Walker on holiday in Greece. They do the kind of things you need to know about: shopping, eating out and getting about. As you will note Tom and Kate speak **Instant Greek** all the time, even to each other. What paragons of virtue!

There are only two things you **must** do:
- Follow the **Day-by-day guide** as suggested. Please don't skip bits and short-change your success. Everything is there for a reason.
- Please buy the recording that accompanies this book. It will also get you to speak faster and with confidence.

When you have filled in your **Certificate** at the end of the book and can speak **Instant Greek**, I would like to hear from you. You can write to me care of Hodder & Stoughton Educational.

Elizabeth Smith

how this book works

Instant Greek has been structured for your rapid success. This is how it works:

Day-by-day guide Stick to it. If you miss a day, add one.

Dialogues Follow Tom and Kate through Greece. The English of Weeks 1–3 is in 'Greek-speak' to get you tuned in.

New words Don't fight them, don't skip them – learn them! The flash cards will help you.

Good news grammar After you read it you are allowed to forget half and still succeed! That's why it's good news.

Flash words and flash sentences Read about these building blocks in the flash card section on page 80. Then use them!

Learn by heart Obligatory! Memorizing puts you on the fast track to speaking in full sentences.

Let's speak Greek *You* will be doing the talking – in Greek.

Spot the keys Listen to rapid Greek and make sense of it.

Say it simply Learn how to use plain, **Instant Greek** to say what you want to say. Don't be shy!

Test your progress Mark your own test and be amazed by the result.

Answers This is where you'll find the answers to the exercises.

▶ This icon asks you to switch on the recording.

Pronunciation If you don't know about it and don't have the recording, go straight to page 15. You need to know about pronunciation before you can start Week 1.

Progress chart Enter your score each week and monitor your progress. Are you going for *very good* or *outstanding*?

Certificate It's on the last page. In six weeks it will have your name on it!

Since **Instant Greek** was first published the euro has become Greece's official currency. Occasionally – as in this book and the recording that goes with it – you will still hear people using drachmas.

At the end of each week record your test score on the progress chart below.

At the end of the course throw out your worst result – anybody can have a bad week – and add up your *five* best weekly scores. Divide the total by five to get your average score and overall course result.

Write your result – *outstanding*, *excellent*, *very good* or *good* – on your **Certificate** at the end of the book. If you scored more than 80% enlarge it and frame it!

Progress chart

90–100%							*outstanding*
80–90%							*excellent*
70–80%							*very good*
60–70%							*good*
Weeks	1	2	3	4	5	6	

Total of five best weeks =

divided by five =

Your final result ______ %

01

week one

Study for 45 minutes – or a little longer if you can!

Day zero

- Start with **Read this first**.
- Read **How this book works**.

Day one

- Read **In the aeroplane**.
- Listen to/Read **Sto aeroplano**.
- Listen to/Read the **New words**, then learn some of them.

Day two

- Repeat **Sto aeroplano** and the **New words**.
- Listen to/Read **Pronunciation**.
- Learn more **New words**.

Day three

- Learn all the **New words** until you know them well.
- Use the **Flash words** to help you.
- Read and learn the **Good news grammar**.

Day four

- Cut out and learn the **Flash sentences**.
- Listen to/Read **Learn by heart**.

Day five

- Listen to/Read **Let's speak Greek**.
- Revise! Tomorrow you'll be testing your progress.

Day six

- Translate **Test your progress**.

Day seven is your day off!

day-by-day guide

In the aeroplane

Tom and Kate Walker are on their way to Greece. They are boarding flight QI 915 to Skiathos via Athens and squeeze past Aristotelis Nikou.

Tom   Excuse me, we have the seats 9a and 9b.

Ari   Yes, sure, one moment please.

Tom   Good morning, we are the Tom and the Kate Walker.

Ari   Good morning, I am the Aristoteles.

Tom   The Aristoteles Onassis?

Ari   No, unfortunately. I am the Aristoteles Nikou.

Tom   We go to Skiathos. And you?

Ari   No, I am going to Athens. But I am from the Patras.

Tom   I was in the Patras in the April. The Patras is very beautiful. I was in the Patras for the company my.

Ari   What do you do?

Tom   I work with computer.

Ari   And you, Mrs Walker? What do you do? Where (do) you work?

Kate   I worked at a school for three years. Now I work at the Rover.

Ari   Are you from the London?

Kate   No, we are from the Manchester. We were one year in the New York and two years in the London. Now we work in the Birmingham.

Ari   I worked for five years at the Fiat. Now I work at the Bank of Greece.

Kate   How is the work at the bank? Good?

Ari   The work is boring. I work a lot but the money is better. I need a lot of money! I have a big house, a Ferrari and four children. The wife my is American. She has a girlfriend in Florida and she is always on the telephone. It costs a lot.

Kate   Now we are on holiday. And you?

Ari   Unfortunately no. Not we are on holiday now. We are on holiday the August. Always we go to Porto Rafti but without the children. We have a house there and not it has telephone!

▶ Sto aeroplano

Tom and Kate Walker are on their way to Greece. They are boarding flight QI 915 to Skiathos via Athens and squeeze past Aristotelis Nikou.

Tom	Signomi, ehume tis thesis enea alpha ke enea vita.
Ari	Ne, vevea, mia stigmi, parakalo.
Tom	Kalimera, imaste o Tom ke i Kate Walker.
Ari	Kalimera, ime o Aristotelis.
Tom	O Aristotelis Onassis?
Ari	Ohi, thistihos. Ime o Aristotelis Nikou.
Tom	Pame stin Skiatho. Ke esis?
Ari	Ohi, pao stin Athina. Ala ime apo tin Patra.
Tom	Imoona stin Patra ton Aprilio. I Patra ine poli omorfi. Imoona stin Patra ya tin eteria moo.
Ari	Ti kanete?
Tom	Thulevo me computer.
Ari	Ke esis, kiria Walker? Ti kanete? Pu thulevete?
Kate	Thulepsa se ena skolio ya tria hronia. Tora thulevo stin Rover.
Ari	Isaste apo to Lonthino?
Kate	Ohi, imaste apo to Manchester. Imastan ena hrono stin Nea Iorki ke thio hronia sto Lonthino. Tora thulevume sto Birmingham.
Ari	Thulepsa ya pende hronia stin Fiat. Tora thulevo stin Trapeza tis Elathos.
Tom	Pos ine i thulia stin trapeza? Kali?
Ari	I thulia ine vareti. Thulevo para poli ala ta lefta ine kalitera. Hriazome pola lefta. Eho ena megalo spiti, mia Ferrari ke tesera pethia. I yineka moo ine Amerikana. Ehi mia fili stin Floritha ke ine sinehia sto tilefono. Kostizi poli.
Kate	Tora imaste se thiakopes. Ke esis?
Ari	Thistihos ohi. Then imaste se thiakopes tora. Imaste se thiakopes ton Avgusto. Panda pame sto Porto Rafti ala horis ta pethia. Ehume ena spiti eki ke then ehi tilefono!

▶ New words

sto aeroplano *in the aeroplane*
signomi *excuse me*
ehume *we have*
o/i/to/ta/tis/tin/ton *the*
thesis *seats*
enea *nine*
alpha, vita *a, b*
ke *and*
ne *yes*
vevea *sure, certain(ly)*
mia stigmi *a/one moment*
parakalo *please*
kalimera *good morning*
imaste *we are, we were/
have been*
ime *I am*
ohi *no*
thistihos *unfortunately*
pame *we/let's go*
sto, stin, stis *to/at/in the*
ke esis *and you?/you, too?*
esis *you*
pao *I go, I'm going*
ala, ma *but*
apo *from*
imoona, imoon *I was*
Aprilis, Aprilio(s) *April*
ine *he/she/it is*
poli *very, much, a lot*
omorfos/i *beautiful*
ya *for*
moo *my*
eteria *company/firm*
ti *what*
kanete *you do/do you do?*
thulevo *I work*
me *with*
kirios, kiria *Mr/gentleman,
Mrs/lady*
pu *where*

thulevete *you work/do you
work?*
thulepsa *I worked*
se *in, at*
enas/mia/ena *a/one*
skolio *school*
tria *three*
hrono, hronia *year, years*
tora *now*
isaste *you are/are you?*
thio *two*
pende *five*
i Trapeza tis Elathos *the Bank
of Greece*
pos *how*
i thulia *the work*
kalos/kali/kalo *good, nice*
varetos/i/o *boring*
poli *a lot, para poli *too much
lefta *money*
kalitera *better*
hriazome *I need*
eho *I have*
megalo *big*
spiti *house*
tesera *four*
pethia *children*
yineka *woman, wife*
Amerikana *American*
ehi *he/she/it has*
fili *(girl)friend*
sinehia *always*
kostizi *it costs*
se thiakopes *on holiday*
then *not*
Avgusto *August*
panda *always*
horis *without*
eki *there*
to tilefono *the telephone*

TOTAL NEW WORDS: 76
...only 295 words to go!

Some easy extras

Meines – months

Ianuarios, Fevruarios, Martios, Aprilios, Maios, Iunios, Iulios, Avgustos, Septemvrios, Octomvrios, Noemvrios, Dekemvrios

Arithmi – numbers

0 = mithen		6 = exi
1 = ena		7 = epta
2 = thio		8 = okto
3 = tria		9 = enea
4 = tesera		10 = theka
5 = pende		

More greetings

kalispera *good evening*; ya/yasu/yasas (pl) *hello, goodbye/'bye*; kalinihta *good night*; adio *goodbye*

▶ Pronunciation

The Greek language is beautiful, so drop all inhibitions and try to speak **Greek** rather than English with the words changed. If Greek pronunciation is new to you **please buy the recording** and listen to the real thing.

As you can see, all the words in **Instant Greek** have been transliterated into phonetic language. That makes it much easier to learn, especially if you are in a hurry. You don't have to learn the Greek script first but can start speaking straight away.

As Greek is a Mediterranean language the vowels in Greek are similar to Italian or Spanish and are explained below. The consonants are pronounced as in English.

You don't have to think too hard about it – just go ahead!

The vowels

The English word in brackets gives you an example of the sound. Say the sound OUT LOUD and then the Greek examples OUT LOUD.

a (star) Amerikana   e (yes) ehi   i (fit) spiti

o (not) pos   u (June) thulia

Stress

In this book, the letter in **bold** type tells you to stress the syllable in which it appears, for example, ehume, parakalo, kiria. Always say the words OUT LOUD. That way you'll remember where the accent goes.

When you go to Greece you'll want to know a little of the script, too. So, as an introduction, here's the Greek alphabet. And later in the course there'll also be a few useful flash words in 'real' Greek script, to help you on your way!

Α Β Γ Δ Ε Ζ Η Θ Ι Κ Λ Μ Ν Ξ Ο Π Ρ Σ Τ Υ Φ Χ Ψ Ω

α β γ δ ε ζ η θ ικ λ μ ν ξ ο π ρ σ τ υ φ χ ψ ω

Good news grammar

This is the good news part of each week. Remember, I promised: no ghastly grammar! I simply explain the differences between Greek and English. This will help you to speak Greek **instantly!**

1 Names of things (nouns)

There are three types of nouns in Greek: *masculine, feminine* and *neuter*.

You can tell which is which by the word o, i or **to** in front of the word.

You can also tell by the ending of the noun:

Most masculine words end in -**os** or -**as**: o yatros (*the doctor*), o anthras (*the man*).

Most feminine words end in -**a** or -**i**: i thulia, mia stigmi.

Most neuter words end in -**o** or -**i**: to tilefono, to spiti.

The adjective describing the noun also ends in -**os** (*masculine*), -**i** (*feminine*) or -**o** (*neuter*). So *the good man, the good work* or *the good house* would be: o kalos anthras, i kali thulia, to kalo spiti.

When you talk about more than one thing (plural) o, i, to change into i, i, ta and the endings of the nouns also change, to -i, -es or -a.

Example: i kali anthres, i kales thulies and ta kala spitia.

This is beginning to sound very complicated, and I don't expect you to learn it or remember it all. You'll pick it up as you go along, without even noticing it! And the best news is, if you muddle things up and make a mistake and say: to kala spitia or o kali anthres, people will not throw a fit but still understand you perfectly well!

2 Doing things (verbs)

Unlike the English, Greeks do not use the *I, you, he, she, it, we* or *they* persons, to identify who is doing something unless they wish to clarify or stress it. So the only way you can tell **who** it is that is doing something is from the **verb itself**. Each person has his, her or its own verb form and ending. Sometimes a verb ending is shared which could lead to some confusion, but amazingly enough it works out all right once it's in a sentence.

There are a few verbs which you'll use every day. I have put the first two of these into a 'gift box' below. Learn them now until you can say them with your eyes closed. It won't take long!

to be		to have	
ime	*I am*	eho	*I have*
isaste	*you are*	ehete	*you have*
ine	*he/she/it is*	ehi	*he/she/it has*
imaste	*we are*	ehume	*we have*
ine	*they are*	ehune	*they have*

3 the Tom, the Kate, the company my

Did you notice? An extra **the** keeps on popping up everywhere in front of nouns and names: Imaste o Tom ke i Kate Walker (*We are the Tom and the Kate Walker*).

When you want to say: *for my company*, you can't just say literally: ya moo eteria. As you will see in the following section, you have to shuffle things around – adding **the** in front of the noun and putting **my** behind the noun – and say:

ya tin eteria moo: *for the company my*

Sounds rather grand doesn't it? ... o Charles; o computer moo.

Moo, soo (sas), too, tis

When Greeks say *my, your, his, her*, they always add **o, i** or **to** depending on whether the word which follows is masculine (male), feminine (female) or neuter (neither male nor female).

So as well as: o computer moo, they say i efimeritha moo, and to autokinito soo.

4 Two into one

Greeks love their language to be as smooth as possible. Little pairs of words like **to the** sound too 'staccato' to them so they 'melt' the two words into one. Here are four examples:

se+to = sto   se+ton = ston   se+tin = stin   se+to = sto

And if you don't 'melt'? No problem. People will still understand you.

▶ Learn by heart

Don't be tempted to skip this exercise because it reminds you of school ... If you want to speak, not stumble, saying a few lines by HEART does the trick!

Learn **Kalimera** by HEART after you have filled in the gaps with your personal, or any, information. Say **Kalimera** aloud and fairly fast. Can you beat 40 seconds?

Kalimera

Kalimera, ime o/i ....*Petros*..................................(*name*)

Ime apo to(n)/ti(n) ....ENGLAND...........................(*place*)

Imoona sto ......SKIATHO......(*place*) ton ....IUNIOS......(*month*)

Thulepsa ya tin .....AUSTIN...................(*firm*) ya thio hronia.

Tora thulevo stin ......SUFFOLK.............................(*place*)

Eho ena megalo spiti stin ....WHATFIELD...(*place*). Kostizi poli.

Ton Avgusto pame sto ......ELATHO..........................(*place*).

Pos ine i Athina ton Aprilio? **O**morfi? ....

▶ Let's speak Greek

Here are ten English sentences. Read each sentence and say it in
Greek – OUT LOUD! Check your answer below before you try
the next sentence. If you have the recording, listen to **Let's speak
Greek** to check your answers.

1 Are you from London?
2 Yes, I am from London.
3 I am on holiday in August.
4 We are going to Corfu (Kerkira).
5 I was in Athens for my firm.

6 Do you have a Ferrari?
7 No – unfortunately!
8 We have a house in Athens.
9 How is the job with Fiat, good?
10 No, it is boring, but the
   money is better.

Well, how many did you get right? If you are not happy do it
again! Here are some questions in Greek. Answer them in
Greek. Start every answer with **Ne**, and talk about yourself.

11 Isaste apo to Manchester?
12 Ehete spiti sto Lonthino?
13 Pame stin Kerkira. Ke esis?
14 Thulevete stin Trapeza tis Elathos?
15 Ehete kali thulia?

Now tell someone in Greek …

16 …that you have two children.
17 …that you were in Athens.
18 …that you have a Fiat Uno.
19 …that you are going to Skiathos.
20 …that Birmingham is boring in November.

Answers

1 Isaste apo to Lonthino?
2 Ne, ime apo to Lonthino.
3 Ime se thiakopes ton Avgusto.
4 Pame stin Kerkira.
5 Imoona stin Athina ya tin eteria moo.
6 Ehete mia Ferrari?
7 Ohi – thistihos.
8 Ehume ena spiti stin Athina.
9 Pos ine i thulia me tin Fiat, kali?
10 Ohi, ine vareti, ala ta hrimata
   ine kalitera.

11 Ne, ime apo to Manchester.
12 Ne, eho spiti sto Lonthino.
13 Ne, ke ego pao stin Kerkira.
14 Ne, thulevo ya tin Trapeza tis
   Elathos.
15 Ne, eho mia kali thulia.
16 Eho thio pethia.
17 Imoona stin Athina.
18 Eho ena Fiat Uno.
19 Pao stin Skiatho.
20 To Birmingham ine vareto
   ton Noemvrio.

Well, what was your score? If you got 20 ticks you can give
yourself a triple star!

Test your progress

This is your only written exercise. You'll be amazed at how easy it is! Translate the 20 sentences without looking at the previous pages.

Don't try to show the stress/accent when you write. That would take you forever!

1   Good morning, we are Ari and Jane.
2   I am from Athens and you?
3   Where (do) you work now?
4   I was in Athens in October.
5   My girlfriend is in Greece for one year.
6   We always go to Rhodes (Rodos) in June.
7   I worked at Fiat in May.
8   What (do) you do in London?
9   I work in an American school.
10 The big house in Porto Rafti is for the children.
11 One moment please, where is Aristotelis?
12 (Does) the house have a telephone? No, unfortunately (not).
13 (Does) a Ferrari cost a lot? Yes, sure, it costs too much.
14 How is the work in Greece, good?
15 Aristotelis has a friend in my firm.
16 We have been in Rhodes for three days.
17 We have good seats in (the) aeroplane.
18 I always have boring holidays.
19 He has a beautiful wife, a Lamborghini and a lot of money …
20 Are you (the) Mrs Onassis? You have a big aeroplane.

When you have finished look up the answers on page 74 and mark your work. Then enter your result on the **Progress Chart** on page 9. If your score is higher than 80% you'll have done very well indeed!

02

week two

Forty-five minutes a day – but a little extra will step up your progress!

Day one

- Read **In Koukounaries**.
- Listen to/Read **Stis Koukounaries**.
- Listen to/Read the **New words**. Learn 20 easy ones.

Day two

- Repeat **Stis Koukounaries** and the **New words**.
- Learn the harder **New words**.
- Use the **Flash words** to help you.

Day three

- Learn all the **New words** until you know them well.
- Read and learn the **Good news grammar**.

Day four

- Cut out and learn the **Flash sentences**.
- Listen to/Read **Learn by heart** (page 30).

Day five

- Listen to/Read **Let's speak Greek** (page 29).
- Go over **Learn by heart**.

Day six

- Translate **Test your progress**.

Day seven is a study-free day!

day-by-day guide

In Koukounaries

In Skiathos Tom and Kate hire a car and drive to Koukounaries. They speak to Anna Pavlithi of 'Hotel Pavlithi' and later, to Andreas, the waiter.

Kate	Good morning. (Do) you have a double room for one night, and no(t) too expensive?
Anna	Yes, we have a room, a little small, with bath and shower. The shower doesn't work, maybe the husband my is able to it fix.
Tom	Where is the room?
Anna	It is here, left. Is it enough big?
Tom	It is a little small but not bad. How much (does) it cost?
Anna	Only 5,000 drachmas for two, but no credit cards! The breakfast is from the eight until nine and half.
Tom	OK. We'll take it. But are we able to have breakfast at eight less quarter? Tomorrow at eight and quarter we want to go to the Ahlathies.
Kate	Excuse me, where can we to drink something? Is there a bar here near?
Anna	There are two bars five minutes from here. It is not difficult. Thirty metres right and then straight on.
(in the bar)	
Andreas	What do you want?
Kate	We want a coffee and a tea with milk.
Andreas	(Do) you want something to eat?
Tom	What (do) you have?
Andreas	We have apple pie or bread rolls.
Kate	Two bread rolls with ham, please.
Tom	The ham not is good.
Kate	The ham my is very good.
Tom	The table is very small.
Kate	But the toilet is big and very clean.
Tom	The tea is cold.
Kate	But the waiter is handsome.
Tom	Waiter! The bill, please!
Andreas	1,500 drachmas, please.

▶ Stis Koukounaries

In Skiathos Tom and Kate hire a car and drive to Koukounaries. They speak to Anna Pavlithi of 'Hotel Pavlithi' and later, to Andreas, the waiter.

Kate	Kalimera. Ehete ena diplo thomatio ya mia nihta ke ohi poli akrivo?
Anna	Ne, ehume ena thomatio, ligo mikro, me banio ke dush. To dush then thulevi, isos o anthras moo bori na to ftiaxi.
Tom	Pu ine to thomatio?
Anna	Ine etho, aristera. Ine arketa megalo?
Tom	Ine ligo mikro, ala ohi ashimo. Poso kostizi?
Anna	Mono pende hiliathes thrahmes ya thio, ala ohi pistotikes kartes! To proino ine apo tis okto mehri tis enea ke misi.
Tom	Entaxi, to pernume. Ala borume na ehume proino stis okto para tetarto? Avrio stis okto ke tetarto thelume na pame stis Ahlathies.
Kate	Signomi, pu borume na piume kati? Ehi kanena bar etho konda?
Anna	Ine thio bar pende lepta apo etho. Then ine thiskolo. Trianda metra thexia ke meta isia.
(sto bar)	
Andreas	Ti thelete?
Kate	Thelume ena kafe ke ena tsai me gala.
Andreas	Thelete kati na fate?
Tom	Ti ehete?
Andreas	Ehume milopita i psomakia.
Kate	Thio psomakia me zabon, parakalo.
Tom	To zabon then ine kalo.
Kate	To zabon moo ine poli kalo.
Tom	To trapezi ine poli mikro.
Kate	Ala i tualeta ine megali ke poli kathari.
Tom	To tsai ine krio.
Kate	Ala o servitoros ine omorfos.
Tom	Servitore! Ton logariasmo, parakalo!
Andreas	Hilies pendakosies thrahmes, parakalo.

▶ New words

Learning words the traditional way can be boring. If you enjoyed the flash cards why not make your own for the rest of the words. Always say the word OUT LOUD. It's the fast track to speaking!

thomatio *room*
thiplo *double*
i nihta *the night*
akrivo *expensive*
ligo *little*
mikro *small*
banio *bath*
dush *shower*
isos *perhaps*
anthras *husband/man*
bori (na) *he/she/it can (is able to)*
na *to (as in to fix)*
ftiaxi *fix/repair*
etho *here*
aristera *left*
arketa *enough*
ohi ashimo *not bad*
poso kostizi *how much does it cost?*
mono *only*
hiliathes *thousands*
drahmes *Greek currency*
pistotikes kartes *credit cards*
proino *breakfast*
mehri *until*
miso/misi *half*
entaxi *OK*
pernume *we take*
borume (na) *we can*
na ehume proino *to have breakfast (we)*
para *less/before (with time)*
ke *and/past (with time)*

tetarto *quarter*
avrio *tomorrow*
thelume (na) *we want/we'd like*
piume *drink (we)*
kati *something*
kanena *none/any (things)*
konda *near*
lepto/lepta *minute, minutes*
thiskolo *difficult*
trianda *30*
metra *metres*
thexia *right*
meta *then*
isia *straight on*
sto bar *in the bar*
ti thelete? *what would you like? (lit. what (do) you want?)*
kafe *coffee*
tsai *tea*
gala *milk*
kati na fate *something to eat*
milopita *apple pie*
i *or*
psomaki, psomakia *bread roll/rolls (little/small bread)*
zabon *ham*
trapezi *table*
i tualeta, tualetes *the toilet(s)*
katharos/i/o *clean*
krios/a/o *cold*
servitoros *waiter*
logariasmos *bill*
pendakosies *500*

TOTAL NEW WORDS: 62
...only 233 words to go!

Some useful extras

Arithmi – more numbers

11 endeka	19 theka-enea	60 exinda
12 thotheka	20 ikosi	70 evthominda
13 thekatria	21 ikosi-ena	80 ogdonda
14 thekatesera	22 ikosi-thio	90 eneninda
15 thekapende	23 ikosi-tria	100 ekato
16 theka-exi	30 trianda	200 thiakosia
17 theka-epta	40 saranda	1000 hilia
18 thekaokto	50 peninda	

I ora – the time

ti ora?   *at what time?*

stis pende?   *at five o'clock?*

ine mia   *it's one o'clock*

ine thio   *it's two o'clock*

ena lepto   *a minute*
        (just a minute)

mia ora   *an hour*

mia mera   *a day*

mia evthomatha   *a week*

enas minas   *a month*

enas hronos   *a year*

too hronu   *next year*

half past = ke misi

quarter past = ke tetarto

quarter to = para tetarto

Good news grammar

1 I, you, he/she/it, we, they

In Greek these are: ego, esis, aftos/afti/afto, emis and afti. As you know they are only used for emphasis: *I do this, you did that*.

Although there is no particular way to know immediately whether afti on its own means *she* or *they*, when it is used in a sentence, it becomes obvious.

Esis is the formal and polite way of saying *you*. When in Greece and speaking **Instant Greek** always use esis. There is also esi for family and friends but that needs a lot more grammar. Leave that till next year!

2 Saying then (not)

Did you notice in Week 1 what happened to the **not** when o Ari Onassis said: 'Then imaste se thiakopes tora?' (**not** we are on holiday now). The **not** moved in front of the verb. It does this all the time:

> I thulia ine kali. I thulia then ine kali. (*The work is good. The work not is good*).

3 Verbs (again)

This week's good news: two more everyday verbs – **go** and **can** – in 'gift boxes', for easy learning. You'll need only a few minutes this time, because there is a bit of a pattern to each verb:

> *I* usually ends in -o: eho, kano, thulevo
> *You* ends in -ete (or -ite): ehete, kanete, thulevete, borite
> *He/she/it* ends in -i: ehi, kani, thulevi
> *We* ends in -ume: ehume, kanume, thulevume
> *They* ends in -un or -une: ehun(e), kanun(e), thulevun(e)

Simple, isn't it?

Here's an example: **kano** (*I do*) in a gift box!

I	*you*	*he/she/it*	*we*	*they*
kano	**kanete**	**kani**	**kanume**	**kanun(e)**

There are a total of 30 verbs in **Instant Greek** and 21 of these are 'regular', which means they follow the above pattern.

That leaves you with nine 'rebels' – verbs which make their own rules. You have learnt two rebels already – **eho** and **ime**, *have* and *be*. Here's one more: **pao** (*go*). Then there's **boro** (*can*) – a regular fellow and member of the good verbs team.

Spend five minutes on each.

pao	*I go*	boro (na)	*I can*
pate	*you go*	borite (na)	*you can*
pai	*he/she/it goes*	bori (na)	*he/she/it can*
pame	*we go*	borume (na)	*we can*
pane	*they go*	borune (na)	*they can*

4 A recap

While you are in the swing of things let's recap on the rest of the regular verbs which you have learnt so far. Once you know how to say I ... *work/fix/take/drink/want (would like)*, you know the pattern, and you can say the rest.

So now take these five on board, too:

> thulevo – ftiahno – perno – pino – thelo

5 A bonus

In Greek the same verbs are used for whether it's an action you **do** or an action you **are doing**. Therefore *I have a house* and *I am having breakfast* would be: eho ena spiti and eho proino. That makes things a lot simpler!

▶ Let's speak Greek

Now let's practise what you have learnt. Here are ten English sentences for you to say in Greek OUT LOUD! After each sentence check to see if you got it right. If you didn't, do the exercise again.

1 We would like a room.
2 At what time is there breakfast?
3 The telephone does not work.
4 How much is (costs) the room?
5 Where is the bar, on the right or on the left?
6 Is there (do you have) something to eat?
7 All right, we take it.
8 Can we go to Athens?
9 We would like to go at half past two.
10 Excuse me, the bill please.

Now answer in Greek. Use **ne** and speak about yourself.

11 Thulevete stis okto ke misi?
12 Thelete ena psomaki?
13 Ehete pola lefta?

Now answer with **ohi** and speak for yourself and a friend.

14 Ehete ena trapezi ya pende?
15 Ehete pende hiliathes thrahmes?
16 Ehete tsai me gala?

And now answer freely. Your answers may differ from mine but still be correct.

17 Pu ine to xenothohio (hotel) Aliki?
18 Pu ine to thomatio?
19 Pu ine to bar?
20 Poso kostizi to tilefono?

Answers

1 Thelume ena thomatio.
2 Ti ora ine to proino?
3 To tilefono then thulevi.
4 Poso kostizi to thomatio?
5 Pu ine to bar, thexia i aristera?
6 Ehete kati na fame?
7 Entaxi, to pernume.
8 Borume na pame stin Athina?
9 Thelume na pame stis thio ke misi.
10 Signomi, ton logariasmo, parakalo.

11 Ne, thulevo stis okto ke misi.
12 Ne, thelo ena psomaki.
13 Ne, eho pola lefta.
14 Ohi, then ehume ena trapezi ya pende.
15 Ohi, then ehume pende hiliathes thrahmes.

16 Ohi, then ehume tsai me gala.
17 To xenothohio Aliki ine stin Patra.
18 Ine thexia ke meta isia.
19 Ine isia ke meta aristera.
20 Kostizi para poli.

▶ Learn by heart

Learn the eight lines **Then eho pola lefta ...** by HEART. Try to say them with a bit of 'drama' in 40 seconds! Choose one of these to fill the gap: o anthras moo, i yineka moo, o filos moo, i fili moo.

Then eho pola lefta ...
Then eho pola lefta ala thelo* na pao thiakopes me ...
Thelume na pame stin Athina me to Rover.
Ine poli omorfi ton Aprilio.
To xenothohio** Pavlithi then ine poli akrivo.
Poso kostizi?
Mono pende hiliathes thrahmes tin nihta.
Borume na pame? Ohi.
Panda ehi poli thulia ke to Rover then thulevi.

---

*thelo: *I would like* **xenothohio: *hotel*

Test your progress

Translate in writing. What do you remember without looking back?

1 Where is (there) a telephone?
2 Excuse me, we only have credit cards.
3 Can we go at seven tomorrow?
4 Do you have (a) enough big table? We are five.
5 The small rooms do not have (a) bath.
6 We would like to eat ham and rolls.
7 We can go from (the) six to (the) quarter to seven.
8 Where can we drink something here near?
9 We were in the bar from nine to half past ten.
10 All right, we take the Rover for a day.
11 How much does the breakfast cost? Only 2,000 drachmas.
12 What (do) you want? The computer? It is not working.
13 How is the apple pie? Good but expensive?
14 Where are the toilets, on the right or on the left?

15 I am going to Hollywood.
16 A coffee, please … we drink too much coffee!
17 Where is (the) Mrs Pavlithi? Perhaps in the bar?
18 One thousand drachmas for a cold tea – it is a little expensive!
19 I was in Rhodes in February. It is not bad.
20 There are 300 bars here, one is (at) 30 metres on the right.

The answers are on page 75. The **Progress chart** awaits your score!

03

week three

Study for 45 minutes a day – but there are no penalties for doing more!

Day one

- Read **We go shopping**.
- Listen to/Read **Pame ya psonia**.
- Listen to/Read the **New words**, then learn some of them.

Day two

- Repeat **Pame ya psonia** and the **New words**.
- Learn all the **New words**. Use the **Flash cards**!

Day three

- Test yourself on all the **New words** – boring, boring, but you are over halfway already!
- Listen to/Read **Spot the keys**.
- Learn the **Good news grammar**.

Day four

- Go over the **Good news grammar**.
- Cut out and learn the ten **Flash sentences**.

Day five

- Listen to/Read **Let's speak Greek**.
- Listen to/Read **Learn by heart**.

Day six

- Go over **Learn by heart**.
- Have a quick look at the **New words**, weeks 1–3.
- You now know over 200 words! Well, more or less.
- Translate **Test your progress**.

Day seven – enjoy your day off!

day-by-day guide

Let's go shopping

Tom and Kate are in Porto Rafti near Athens. They have rented a summer apartment for a week. Kate plans to do some shopping, but Tom has other ideas ...

Kate Today we must do the shopping. Let's go into the centre with the bus.

Tom But there is bad weather, it does cold and there is a lot of sport on television – the golf at two and a half.

Kate I am sorry, but we must go first to the cash dispenser and to the post office or kiosk for stamps ... then to the chemist's and to the dry cleaner's.

Tom In that case no golf ... perhaps the football at four and a quarter. This is all?

Kate No, we have to go to a department store to buy a new suitcase. Then I have to go to the supermarket and to the hairdresser's. And afterwards I want to buy shoes.

Tom Good grief! Until when are the shops open?

Kate Until the seven and half, I believe.

Tom Then no football ... perhaps the tennis at the eight.

(*Later*)

Kate Hello Tom, here is the shopping: 200g ham, a piece cheese, half a kilo apples, two kilos potatoes, feta cheese, sugar, bread, butter, some eggs, six beers and a bottle (of) wine. I have bought too many things.

Tom It doesn't matter. Yesterday we not ate much. And what is in the big bag? Something for me?

Kate Well, near to the Minion there was a small shop and I saw some shoes which were the number (size) my. Not are they beautiful? White and blue. The sales assistant was very nice and handsome like the Tom Cruise.

Tom Who is the Tom Cruise? And how much cost the shoes?

Kate They were a little expensive, but they cost the same in the England – 300,000 drachmas.

Tom What? The wife my crazy!

Kate But this the T-shirt for the golf was very cheap. Size 42, only 25,000 drachmas. Here is a newspaper in the English and now not has tennis in the TV?

▶ Pame ya psonia

Tom and Kate are in Porto Rafti near Athens. They have rented a summer apartment for a week. Kate plans to do some shopping, but Tom has other ideas …

Kate Simera prepi na kanume ta psonia. Pame sto kendro me to leoforio.

Tom Ma o keros ine kakos, kani krio ke ehi poli spor stin tileorasi – to golf stis thio ke misi.

Kate Lipame, ala prepi na pame prota stin mihani analipsis ke sto tahithromio i sto periptero ya gramatosima … meta sto farmakio ke sto stegnokatharistirio.

Tom Etsi, ohi golf … isos to pothosfero stis teseris ke tetarto. Afto ine olo?

Kate Ohi, prepi na pame se ena polikatastima na agorasume mia kenooryia valitsa. Meta prepi na pao sto supermarket ke sto komotirio. Ke meta thelo na agoraso paputsia.

Tom Thee moo. Mehri pote ine ta magazia anihta?

Kate Mehri tis epta ke misi, pistevo.

Tom Etsi ohi pothosfero … isos to tenis stis okto.
(*Argotera*)

Kate Yasu Tom, etho ine ta psonia: thiakosia gramaria zabon, ena komati tiri, miso kilo mila, thio kila patates, feta, zahari, psomi, vootiro, merika avga, exi bires ke ena bookali krasi. Agorasa para pola pragmata.

Tom Then pirazi. Hthes then fagame poli. Ke ti ine stin megali tsanda? Kati ya mena?

Kate Lipon, konda sto Minion itan ena mikro magazi ke itha kati paputsia pu itan sto numero moo. Then ine omorfa? Aspra ke ble. O politis itan poli kalos ke omorfos san ton Tom Cruise.

Tom Pios ine o Tom Cruise? Ke poso kostisan ta paputsia?

Kate Itan ligo pio akriva, ala kostizoon to ithio stin Anglia – triakosies hiliathes thrahmes.

Tom Ti? I yineka moo ine treli.

Kate Ala afto to bloozaki ya to golf itan poli ftino. Numero saranda-thio, mono ikosipende hiliathes thrahmes. Etho ine mia efimeritha sta Anglika, ke tora then ehi tenis stin tileorasi?

▶ New words

Learn the **New words** in half the time using flash cards. There are 18 to start you off. Get a friend to make the rest!

ta psonia   *the shopping*
simera   *today*
prepi na   *we must*
kanume   *do (we)*
kendro   *centre*
leoforio   *bus*
keros   *weather; time*
kakos   *bad*
kani krio   *it is cold*
    (lit. it does cold)
i tileorasi   *the television*
lipame   *I'm sorry*
prota   *first*
mihani analipsis   *cash machine*
tahithromio   *post office*
periptero   *kiosk (it sells stamps)*
meta   *then, afterwards*
gramatosima   *stamps*
farmakio   *chemist's*
stegnokatharistirio   *dry cleaner's*
etsi   *therefore, in that case*
pothosfero   *football*
afto   *this*
olos, oli, olo, oli, oles, ola   *all*
polikatastima   *department store*
agorasume   *buy (we)*
kenooryios/a/o   *new*
valitsa   *suitcase*
to komotirio   *the hairdresser's*
thelo   *I want*
magazi(a)   *shop(s)*
agoraso   *buy (I)*
ta paputsia   *the shoes*
thee moo   *good grief!*
pote   *when?*
anihta   *open*
pistevo   *I believe/think*
argotera   *later*
gramaria   *grams*

komati   *piece*
tiri   *cheese*
kilo   *kilo*
patates   *potatoes*
zahari   *sugar*
psomi   *bread*
vootiro   *butter*
merika   *some*
avgo, avga   *egg, eggs*
bira, bires   *beer, beers*
bookali   *bottle*
krasi   *wine*
agorasa   *I bought, I have bought*
para pola   *too many*
pragma, pragmata   *thing, things*
then pirazi   *it doesn't matter*
hthes   *yesterday*
fagame   *we ate, have eaten*
tsanda   *bag*
emena   *me*
lipon   *well ...*
to Minion   *a well-known Greek department store*
itan   *was/were*
itha   *I saw*
numero   *size, number*
aspra   *white*
ble   *blue*
politis   *sales assistant*
san   *like*
pios?, pia?, pio?; pu   *who?, which*
kostizoon   *they cost*
to ithio   *the same*
Anglia   *England*
treli   *crazy*
bloozaki   *T-shirt*

ftino   cheap   Anglik**os/i/a**   English
mia efimeritha   a newspaper

> **TOTAL NEW WORDS: 76**
> **...only 157 words to go!**

More extras

Ta hromata – colours

aspro	white	kitrino	yellow
mavro	black	kafe	brown
kokino	red	gri	grey
ble	blue	portokali	orange
prasino	green	roz	pink

▶ Spot the keys

By now you can say many things in Greek. But what happens if
you ask a question and don't understand the answer – hitting you
at the speed of an automatic rifle? The smart way is not to panic,
but to listen only for the words you know. Any familiar words
which you pick up will provide you with key words – clues to
what the other person is saying. If you have the recording, listen
to the following dialogue. If you don't – read on.

You are trying to ask the way to the post office ...

You   Signomi, pu ine to tahithromio parakalo?
Answer   To tahithromio then ine etho konda. *Na* to *vris*
              prepi *napas* sto *telostoothromukenaprohorisisya
              enamiliperipu.* Eki *stripse* thexia ke ine konda se
              ena polikatastima *san* to Minion. Thexia ine ena ble
              magazi ke *apenandi* ine i trapeza. Eki ine to
              tahithromio!

Can you find your way with the key words? I think you'll get
there!

Good news grammar

1 Doing more things with verbs: the past

To talk about something that happened before or in the past in Greek, you need to change the verb. This happens in two stages: First you learn the pattern in Greek for *I did*, or *I went*, or *I could* and then you learn the pattern for the other verb endings. Remember the endings of the present tense? **-o-ete/ite, -i, -ume** and **-un(e)**? For the past tense it's **-a, -ate, -e, -ame** and **-an(e)**. Look at the pattern for 'buy':

I bought	agoras-a	*we bought*	agoras-ame
you bought	agoras-ate	*they bought*	agoras-ane
he/she/it bought	agoras-e		

Spend a couple of minutes on these every day until you know them in your sleep. If all fails stick them on the fridge!

Among the 30 **Instant** verbs there's one 'rebel', one that's different in the past tense. So you'd better learn it straight away:

I was	*you were*	*he/she/it was*	*we were*	*they were*
imoona	isaste	itan	imaste	itan(e)

Here are some more everyday verbs which you'll need both in the present and in the past – now you know how it's done.

I have	eho	*I had*	iha
I do	kano	*I did*	ekana
I go	pao	*I went*	piga
I work	thulevo	*I worked*	thulepsa
I need	hriazome	*I needed*	hriastika
I can	boro	*I could*	boresa
I fix	ftiahno	*I fixed*	eftiaxa
I eat	troo	*I ate*	efaga
I take	perno	*I took*	pira
I want	thelo	*I wanted*	ithela
I think/believe	pistevo	*I thought*	pistepsa
I see	vlepo	*I saw*	itha

Phew! That's quite a list! Take a few minutes *every day* to learn these – don't try it in one go.

The ones starting with an **e** sometimes lose it along the line (ekana, but kanate), but don't worry about it.

2 *na* (to): makes sense

Prepi na pao: (*I must (to) go*). Borume na pame (*we can (to) go*).
So what is the **na** (to) doing there? Think of *must* as *have to* and
of *can* as *are able to* ... and it makes sense!

▶ Let's speak Greek

Over to you! Cover up the answers below. Always answer OUT
LOUD! Start with a ten-point warm-up. Say in Greek:

1 Now we must go.
2 I want to do the shopping.
3 Are the shops open?
4 I am sorry, but it is very expensive.
5 Is there a bus for the centre?
6 We ate at the Taverna Aliki.
7 Can we buy wine at the supermarket?
8 It costs thirty-seven thousand drachmas.
9 We have been here from three to half past four.
10 Good grief, the wine was expensive!

Answer in Greek using **Ohi**. Speak about yourself.

11 Hriazeste mia mihani analipsis?
12 Ehi pothosfero stin tileorasi?
13 Agorasate tipota sto farmakio?

Answer in Greek using the words in brackets.

14 Ti agorasate?   (tipota = *nothing*)
15 Pote pigenete (*go*) sto pothosfero?   (simera, stis thio)
16 Mehri pote ine anihta ta magazia?   (mehri tis exi)
17 Pios efage para poli?   (Emis, fagame)
18 Pu ithate tin valitsa?   (itha, magazi)
19 Agorasate gramatosima etho?   (ohi, sto tahithromio)
20 Ti kero kani simera?   (kani krio, simera)

Answers

1 Tora prepi na pame.
2 Thelo na kano ta psonia.
3 Ine ta magazia anihta?
4 Lipame, ala ine poli akrivo.
5 Ehi leoforio ya to kendro?
6 Fagame stin taverna Aliki.
7 Borume na agorasume krasi sto
    supermarket?

8 Kostizi trianda-epta hiliathes
    thrahmes.
9 Imaste etho apo tis tris mehri tis
    teseris ke misi.
10 Thee moo, to krasi itan akrivo!
11 Ohi then hriazome mia mihani
    analipsis.

12 Ohi then ehi pothosfero stin tileorasi.
13 Ohi then agorasa tipota sto farmakio.
14 Then agorasa tipota.
15 Piyeno sto pothosfero simera stis thio.

16 Ta magazia ine anihta mehri tis exi.
17 Emis fagame para poli.
18 Itha tin valitsa se ena magazi.
19 Ohi, then agorasa ta gramatosima sto tahithromio.
20 O keros ine kakos. Kani krio simera.

▶ Learn by heart

Say this dialogue in under a minute and with a lot of expression!

Pame ya psonia

Pame ya psonia … thee moo!

Tom Simera kani krio. Ehi pothosfero stin tileorasi.

Kate Lipame ala prepi na kanume ta psonia. Then ehume tipota* na fame. Prepi na pame prota stin mihani analipsis, ke meta sto supermarket.

(*argotera*)

Kate Etho ine ta psonia! Agorasa pola: zabon, tiri, psomi ke gramatosima ya tin Anglia.

Tom Kati ya mena? Ohi bira? Ohi krasi? Tipota ya mena? Thee moo!

---

*tipota: *nothing*

Test your progress

Translate in writing. Then check your answers on page 75 and be amazed!

1 First I want to go to the cash dispenser.
2 In this the shop the shoes cost too much.
3 Did you see my husband in the chemist's?
4 We were here until a quarter past ten.
5 We saw the tennis in England on (in) television.
6 I am sorry, but we do not have the same in red, in size (number) 44.
7 This the shop is not cheap.
8 Who repaired my telephone? You?
9 Here is the department store. But it is not open.
10 Today we did not buy too many things. Only bread and half a kilo (of) butter.
11 I ate everything – eggs, apples, potatoes and a piece (of) cheese.
12 We must do the shopping. Is this the centre?
13 Yesterday I was in the office (firm) until nine o'clock.

14 The English newspapers cost a lot in Greece.
15 Is there a bus? No? It does not matter.
16 He was a very nice sales assistant.
17 What is this? Something for me?
18 Did she buy the bag near here or at MINION?
19 Everything was very expensive. Therefore I did not buy anything.
20 We need three kilos, I believe.

Remember the **Progress chart**? You are now halfway there!

04

week four

Study for 45 minutes a day – but if you are keen try 50 or 55!

Day one

- Read **Let's go and eat**.
- Listen to/Read **Pame na fame**.
- Listen to/Read the **New words**. Learn the easy ones.

Day two

- Repeat the dialogue. Learn the harder **New words**.
- Cut out the **Flash words** to help you.

Day three

- Learn all the **New words** until you know them well.
- Read and learn the **Good news grammar**.

Day four

- Listen to/Read **Learn by heart**.
- Cut out and learn the ten **Flash sentences**.

Day five

- Read **Say it simply**.
- Listen to/Read **Let's speak Greek**.

Day six

- Listen to/Read **Spot the keys**.
- Translate **Test your progress**.

Day seven

Are you keeping your scores above 60%? In that case ...
have a good day off!

day-by-day guide

Let's go and eat

Tom and Kate are back in Athens. Pavlos Thiamadis invites them to dinner.

Kate   Tom, someone has telephoned. He did not say why. Mister Thiamadis from Thesaloniki. Here is the number.

Tom   Ah yes, Pavlos Thiamadis, a good client. His firm is in Thesaloniki. I know him well. He is very nice. I have an appointment with him on Thursday. It is important.

Tom   *(Telephones)* Hello! Good morning Mr Thiamadis. I am Tom Walker ... Yes, thank you ... yes, sure, it is possible ... of course ... next week, very interesting ... no, we have time. Wonderful! No, only two days ... ah yes ... when? Tonight, at eight ... upstairs, by the exit ... in front of the door. All right! In that case, until tonight, thank you very much, goodbye.

Kate   What are we doing tonight?

Tom   We are eating with Mr Thiamadis. In the centre, behind the church. He says that it is a new and very good restaurant. Mr Thiamadis is for three days in Athens with Edith and Peter Palmer from our company.

Kate   I know Edith Palmer. She is boring and thinks that she knows everything. She has a terrible dog. Well ... I believe I am sick. I have a bad cold and pains. I need a doctor.

Tom   No, please! It's not possible! Mr Thiamadis is very important.

(At the restaurant) Anthreas, the head waiter, explains the menu.

Anthreas   The fish is not on the menu and for dessert today there is baklavas or ice cream.

Pavlos   Mrs Walker, can I help you? Perhaps a suvlaki and afterwards a salad and fish?

Kate   A steak with salad, please.

Edith   A steak, Kate? It is too much red meat.

Pavlos   And you, Mr Walker, what would you like? And what do you want to drink?

Tom   A jumbo suvlaki with chips and vegetables and a beer, please.

Edith   The vegetables have a lot of oil, Tom.

⸺➤ Page 46

▶ Pame na fame

Tom and Kate are back in Athens. Pavlos Thiamadis invites them to dinner.

Kate   Tom, kapios tilefonise. Then ipe yati. O kirios Thiamadis apo tin Thesaloniki. Etho ine to numero.

Tom   Ah, ne, o Pavlos Thiamadis, ena kalos pelatis. I eteria too ine stin Thesaloniki. Ton xero kala. Ine poli kalos. Eho ena randevu mazi too tin Pempti. Ine simandiko.

Tom   *(Tilefoni)* Parakalo! Kalimera, kirie Thiamadi. Ime o Tom Walker ... Ne, efharisto ... ne, vevea, ine thinaton ... fisika ... tin epomeni evthomatha, poli enthiaferon ... ohi, ehume kero. Exoha! Ohi, mono thio meres ... ah ne ... pote? Apopse, stis okto ... epano, thipla stin exotho ... brosta stin porta. Endaxi! Etsi, apopse, efharisto poli, adio.

Kate   Ti kanume apopse?

Tom   Trome me ton kirio Thiamadi. Sto kendro, piso apo tin eklisia. Lei oti ine kenuryio ke ena poli kalo estiatorio. O kirios Thiamadis ine ya tris meres stin Athina me tin Edith ke ton Peter Palmer apo tin eteria mas.

Kate   Xero tin Edith Palmer. Ine vareti ke pistevi oti ta xeri ola. Ehi enan apesio skiio. Lipon ... pistevo oti ime arosti. Eho ena kako krio ke pono. Hriazome ena yatro.

Tom   Ohi, se parakalo. Then ine thinaton! O kirios Thiamadis ine poli simandikos.

(Sto estiatorio) Anthreas, the head waiter, explains the menu.

Anthreas   To psari then ine sto menoo ke ya epithorpio simera ehume baklava i pagoto.

Pavlos   Kiria Walker, boro na sas voithiso? Isos ena suvlaki ke meta mia salata ke psari?

Kate   Mia brizola me salata, parakalo.

Edith   Brizola, Kate? Para poli kokino kreas.

Pavlos   Ke esis, kirie Walker, ti thelete? Ke ti thelete na pieite.

Tom   Ena megalo suvlaki me patates tiganites ke lahanika ke mia bira, parakalo.

Edith   Ta lahanika ehune poli lathi, Tom.

⋯⟶ Page 47

Pavlos	And you, Mrs Palmer?
Edith	I want a little grilled chicken and a glass of water, please.
(*Later*)	
Pavlos	Are we having fruit, or perhaps better – the baklava? No? Nothing? Have we finished? A coffee for someone? Nobody? Well … It is late. The bill, please.
Edith	Mr Thiamadis, can you help me please? How do they say 'doggy bag' in Greek? I want a little meat for my dog.
Kate	But Edith, the dog is in England!

▶ New words

kapios, kapion *someone*
tilefonise *(has) telephoned*
ipe *he/she/it said*
yati *why*
pelatis *client*
xero *I know*
kala *well*
randevu *appointment*
mazi too *with him*
Pempti *Thursday*
simandiko *important*
parakalo *not at all (and what you say when answering the phone)*
efharisto/efharisto poli *thank you/thank you very much*
thinaton *possible*
fisika *of course/naturally*
tin epomeni evthomatha *next week*
enthiaferon *interesting*
kero *time*
exoha *wonderful*
apopse *tonight*
epano *up/upstairs*
thipla *by, next to*
exothos *exit*

brosta *in front of*
porta *door*
endaxi *all right, OK*
trome *we eat*
piso apo *behind*
eklisia *church*
lei *he/she/it says*
oti *that*
estiatorio *restaurant*
mas *our*
pistevi *he/she/it believes*
xeri *he/she/it knows*
apesio *terrible*
skilos *dog*
arosti *sick*
krio *cold/flu*
pono *or* pono *pain or hurts*
yatros *doctor*
psari *fish*
menoo *menu*
epithorpio *dessert*
baklava *famous Greek pastry*
pagoto *ice cream*
voithiso *to help*
suvlaki *Greek meat dish (like shish kebab)*
salata *salad*

Pavlos	Ke esis, kiria Palmer?
Edith	Thelo kotopulo psito ke ena potiri nero, parakalo.
(Argotera)	
Pavlos	Thelume fruta, i isos kati kalitero – baklava? **O**hi? Tipota? Teliosame? Kafe ya kapion? Kanis? Lipon … ine arga. Ton logariasmo, parakalo.
Edith	Kirie Thiamadi, borite na me voithisete, parakalo? Pos lene 'doggy bag' sta Elinika? Thelo ligo kreas ya ton skilo moo.
Kate	Ma Edith, o skilos ine stin Anglia!

kreas   *meat*
brizola   *steak*
(na) pieite   *to drink*
patates tiganites   *chips*
lahanika   *vegetables*
lathi   *oil*
kotopulo   *chicken*
psito   *grilled*
potiri   *glass*
nero   *water*

fruta   *fruit*
teliosame   *we've finished/ we finished*
kanis   *nobody/anyone*
arga   *late; slow(ly)*
borite na me voithisete   *can you help me?*
Pos to lene sta Elinika …   *How do you say in Greek …?*

**TOTAL NEW WORDS: 65
…only 92 words to go!**

Last easy extras

Days of the week – *meres tis evthomathas*

Theftera	*Monday*	Paraskevi	*Friday*
Triti	*Tuesday*	Savato	*Saturday*
Tetarti	*Wednesday*	Kiriaki	*Sunday*
Pempti	*Thursday*		

Good news grammar

1 Verbs again

Here are the new verbs that appeared in the dialogue in Week 4. Once again I'll give you both the present and the past as the base for your mental acrobatics.

I say	leo*	I said	ipa
I know	xero	I knew	ixera
I help	voitho	I helped	voithisa
I phone	tilefono	I phoned	tilefonisa

*leo is a rebel. Look him up on page 71 and shudder.

Four pairs – eight minutes to learn. And then you can say a whole lot more, such as – what you said, whom you phoned, and what you knew ... Go for it!

And more good news, if you ever get confused or forget: there's a complete summary of verbs in Week 6 **Good news grammar**. Have a sneak preview! You'll know most of these in three weeks' time!

And if all fails you can always say 'Pos lene sta Elinika ...?' And everyone will be rushing to help.

2 'it', 'her', 'him' and 'them'

Imagine you're talking about certain things – wine, the company, holidays or seats on the plane, or certain people – Tom, Kate, a client. Now imagine you are just referring to these things, or people without actually saying their name. You would say *it* or *them*.

In Greek *it*, *her*, *him* are **ton, tin, to** and *them* is **tous, tis, ta**, depending on the word you are referring to.

Agorazo to krasi → to agorazo (*I buy it*)
Agorazo tin bira → tin agorazo (*I buy it*)
Agorazo ta paputsia → ta agorazo (*I buy them*)
Ehi thiakopes ton Aprilio → tis ehi ton Aprilio
(*he has them in April*)
Ehume ta grammatosima → ta ehume (*we have them*)

Did you notice? ... the *it* or *them* always goes in front of the verb; *It I buy, It you buy, Them we have.*

3 'think' and 'know'

Here are two more everyday verbs which deserve some extra attention. By now you know the sequence: it's always *I – you – he/she/it – we – they*. So this time the gift boxes are quite thin:

know: **xero**

now:	xero	xerete	xeri	xerume	xerun(e)
yesterday:	ixera	xerate	ixere	xerame	xerane

think/believe: **pistevo**

today		last year	
pistevo	pistevume	pistepsa	pistepsame
pistevete	pistevun(e	pistepsate	pistepsan(e)
pistevi		pistepse	

4 Attention!

Here's something unusual and different from other languages: when you want to say in Greek *he can go* you actually say: *he can goes* – **bori na pai**. When the two verbs come together: *able to + go* or *want to + go*, note they both take the same ending.

Borume na pame. Thelo na pao.

5 Best news: *prepi na* – must/have to

Prepi na never changes: no endings to learn! *I must, you must, we must* … It's always **prepi na**. If you want to make sure *who must* you can add the person: ego, emis, esis, etc. … easy!

▶ Learn by heart

Here is a short piece about someone who is rather fed up. Put yourself in his shoes … Learn it and act it out in under 50 seconds.

A Xerete ton kirio Adoni? Tilefonise tora. Theli na fao mazi too.
B Yati?
A Ine enas simandikos pelatis. Mono pu then ine kalos. Troi ke pini para poli.
B Ke pote?
A Apopse! Ehi pothosfero stin tileorasi. Thelo na po* oti ime arostos ala then boro … panda** i eteria! Thee moo!
B Aah … Lipame.

---

*po: *say* **panda: *always*

Say it simply

When people want to speak Greek but don't dare, it's usually because they are trying to translate what they want to say from English into Greek. And because they don't know some of the words they give up!

With **Instant Greek** you work around the words you don't know with the words you do know! And believe me, 371 words are enough to say anything! It may not always be very elegant, but who cares? You are speaking and communicating!

Here are three examples, showing you how to say things in a simple way. The English words which are not part of the **Instant** vocabulary are in **bold**.

1 You need to **change your flight** to London from Tuesday to Friday.

   This is what you could say – simply:

   Thelo na paro to aeroplano ya to Lonthino tin Paraskevi, ohi tin Triti.

2 You want to get your **purse** and **mobile phone** from the **coach** which the driver has locked.

   Say it simply:

   Signomi. Prepi na paro ta hrimata moo ke to mikro tilefono apo to leoforio.

3 This time your friend has **broken the heel** of her **only pair of** shoes. You have to **catch** a plane and need some help now.

   This is what you could say:

   Signomi, ta paputsia tis filis moo then ine entaxi.
   Prepi na ta ftiaxume ke na pame sto aeroplano. Hriazome voithia tora.

▶ Let's speak Greek

Here are eight sentences to say in Greek, and then on to greater things!

1 I am sorry, I do not have time.
2 Are we going with him?
3 I want (would like) a salad.
4 We were here yesterday.
5 Excuse me, what did you say?
6 I did not take it.
7 When did you work in Greece?
8 We did not do anything.

Now pretend you are in Greece with English friends who do not speak Greek. They will want you to ask people things and will want you to do it for them in Greek. They will say: 'Please ask him ...'. Start with **Signomi** ...

9 if he knows Mr Thiamadis.
10 where he bought the stamps.
11 if he has an appointment now.
12 where the restaurant is.

Now your friends will ask you to tell people things. They use some words which you don't know, so you have to use **Instant** words. They will say: 'Please tell her that ...'. Start your sentence with **Lipame** ...

13 her suvlaki is cold.
14 we are having only water, no wine.
15 she is a vegetarian.
16 he does not have the number.

While shopping you are offered various items. You take them all, saying 'yes, I take it' or 'yes, I take him'.

17 ta fruta?   19 tin bira?
18 to pagoto?   20 ton skilo?

Answers

1 Lipame, then eho kero.
2 Pame mazi too?
3 Thelo mia salata.
4 Imaste etho hthes.
5 Signomi, ti ipate?
6 Then to pira.
7 Pote thulepsate stin Elatha?
8 Then kaname tipota.
9 Signomi, xerete ton kirio Thiamadi?
10 Signomi, pu agorasate ta gramatosima?
11 Signomi, ehete ena randevu tora?
12 Signomi, pu ine to estiatorio?
13 Lipame, to suvlaki sas ine krio.
14 Lipame, ehume mono nero, ohi krasi.
15 Lipame, then troi kreas.
16 Lipame, then ehi to numero.
17 Ne, ta perno.
18 Ne, to perno.
19 Ne, tin perno.
20 Ne, ton perno.

▶ Spot the keys

You practised listening for key words when you asked the way
to the post office in Week 3. Now you are in a department store.
You have asked the sales assistant if the black dress you liked is
also available in size 44 (Greek). She said: 'Ohi, mia stigmi,
parakalo ...' and disappeared. When she came back this is what
she said:

Thistihos ehume numero saranda-tesera mono se prasino.
Then ehume kanena mavro forema se afto to meyethos. Ala
ehume *mavra foremata* se numero saranda-thio *yati poli
pelates zitune afto* to *meyethos.* To numero saranda-thio
mavro-pistevo, ine arketa megalo *ya sas.*

It appears that size 44 was only available in green but she
believes that size 42 might be big enough.

Test your progress

1 Has someone telephoned Mr Thiamadis?
2 I want to know where the restaurant is.
3 It is late and he is not there. What are we doing tonight?
4 Here is the menu! Do you know the wines of Ahaia?
5 The cash dispenser is upstairs, behind the exit, near the door.
6 Wednesday we must go to the doctor. It is an important
   appointment.
7 Why do I say she is boring? Because I know her well.
8 Did you see him? I must go to Larisa with him.
9 Mr Thiamadis is my client. He has bought everything.
10 I want to buy this thing. How does one say in Greek ...?
11 Next week? I am sorry. It is not possible.
12 Can you help me please? Many thanks!
13 One hundred thousand drachmas for two days. Very
   interesting. Yes, of course we take it.
14 I must buy three things for my friends.
15 I have a cold. I need a doctor.
16 Can they eat only the baklava?
17 There is a terrible dog. What can we do?
18 Nobody saw who ate the steak.
19 Can I say something: the chicken is not bad but the fish is
   better.
20 What do you take? The fruit? Yes, sure, it is from Ahaia.

How are your 'shares' looking on the **Progress chart**? Going up?

05

week five

How about 15 minutes on the train, tube or bus, 10 minutes on the way home and 20 minutes before switching on the television ...?

Day one

- Read **On the move**.
- Listen to/Read **Taxithevondas**.
- Listen to/Read the **New words**. Learn 15 or more.

Day two

- Repeat the dialogue. Learn the harder **New words**.
- Cut out the **Flash words** to get stuck in.

Day three

- Test yourself to perfection on all the **New words**.
- Read and learn the **Good news grammar** (page 60).

Day four (the tough day)

- Listen to/Read **Learn by heart** (page 59).
- Cut out and learn the ten **Flash sentences**.

Day five

- Listen to/Read **Let's speak Greek**.
- Go over **Learn by heart**.

Day six

- Listen to/Read **Spot the keys**.
- Translate **Test your progress**.

Day seven

I bet you don't want a day off ... but I insist!

day-by-day guide

On the move

Tom and Kate are travelling through Southern Greece – by train, bus and hire car. They talk to Anna, the ticket clerk at the station, to Jim on the train and later to Antonis, the bus driver.

At the station

Tom   Two tickets for Patras, please.

Anna   Thereandback?

Tom   There and what? Can you speak more slowly, please?

Anna   There – and – back?

Tom   No, one way only. What time is there a train and from which platform?

Anna   At four minutes to ten. Platform eight.

Kate   Quickly, Tom, here are two seats, non-smoking. Oh, but someone is smoking. Excuse me, you cannot smoke, because it is non-smoking here. It is forbidden to smoke.

Jim   I am sorry. I don't understand, I speak only English.

At the bus stop

Kate   There is no bus. We have to wait 20 minutes. Tom, here are my postcards. Over there is a letter-box. I want to take some photos. The town is beautiful in the sun.

Tom   Kate, come on! There are a lot of people. Here are two buses! Both are blue. This one is full. Let's take the other one. (*on the bus*) Two for Sparta, please.

Antonis This bus goes only to Corinth.

Tom   But we are in Corinth!

Antonis Yes, yes, but this is the bus for the hospital of Corinth.

In the car

Tom   Here is our car. Only 50,000 drachmas for three days. I am very satisfied.

Kate   I do not like the car. It costs so little because it's very old. Let's hope that we don't have problems.

Tom   I am sorry. The first car was too expensive and the second (one) too big. This was the last one.

         (*Later*) Where are we? There is no map! On the left there is a petrol station, and on the right there is a school. Hurry up!

⸬⸬⸬➡ Page 58

▶ Taxithevondas

Tom and Kate are travelling through Southern Greece – by train, bus and hire car. They talk to Anna, the ticket clerk at the station, to Jim on the train and later to Antonis, the bus driver.

Ston stathmo

Tom	Thio isitiria ya tin Patra, parakalo.
Anna	Me-epistrofi?
Tom	Me ti? Borite na milisete pio arga, parakalo?
Anna	Me epistrofi?
Tom	Ohi, mono mias katefthinsis. Ti ora ehi ena treno ke apo pia platforma?
Anna	Stis tesseris para theka. Platforma okto.
Kate	Grigora Tom, etho ine thio thesis, ya mi kapnizodes. Ah, ala kapios kapnizi. Signomi, then borite na kapnisete, ine ya mi kapnizodes etho. Apagorevete to kapnisma.
Jim	Sorry, I don't understand, milao only Anglika.

Stin stasi leoforiou

Kate	Then ehi leoforio. Prepi na perimenume ikosi lepta. Tom, etho ine ta kart-postal moo. Eki pera ine ena gramatokivotio. Thelo na paro merikes fotografies. I poli ine poli omorfi ston ilio.
Tom	Kate, ela! Ehi poli kosmo. Etho ine thio leoforia! Ke ta thio ine ble. Afto ine yemato. As parume to alo.
	(sto leoforio) Thio ya Sparti, parakalo.
Antonis	Afto to leoforio pai mono stin Korintho.
Tom	Ma imaste stin Korintho!
Antonis	Ne, ne, ala afto ine to leoforio ya to nosokomio tis Korinthu.

Sto aftokinito

Tom	Etho ine to aftokinito mas. Mono peninda hiliathes thrahmes ya tris meres. Ime poli ikanopioimenos.
Kate	Then moo aresi to aftokinito. Kostizi toso ligo yati ine poli palio. As elpisume oti then tha ehume kanena provlima.
Tom	Lipame. To proto aftokinito itan poli akrivo ke to theftero poli megalo. Afto itan to telefteo.
	(Argotera) Pu imaste? Then ehi harti! Aristera ine ena venzinathiko ke thexia ine ena skolio. Kane grigora!

⸺▶ Page 59

Kate   We are coming from the underground station. The main road is at the (traffic) lights. It's perhaps three kilometres until the motorway. *(On the motorway)* Why does the car go slowly? Have we enough petrol? How many litres? Do we have oil? Is the engine too hot? The car is a wreck. Where is the mobile phone? Where is the number of the garage? Where is my bag?

Tom   Kate, please! I have a headache. And now it's raining! And why are the police behind us?

▶ New words

taxithevondas   *on the move/ travelling*
stathmos   *railway station*
isitirio   *ticket*
me epistrofi   *(with) return*
mias katefthinsis   *one way*
borite na milisete   *can you speak*
pio   *more*
treno   *train*
pios, pia, pio   *who, which*
platforma   *platform*
(grigora   *quickly*)
mi kapnizodes   *non-smoking*
kapnizi   *he/she/it smokes*
apagorevete to kapnisma   *it's forbidden to smoke*
then katalaveno   *I don't understand*
milao   *I speak*
stasi   *bus stop*
perimeno   *I wait*
kart-postal   *postcard*
eki pera   *over there*
gramatokivotio   *letter-box*
fotografia   *photograph*
poli   *city/town*
ilios   *the sun*
ehi kosmo   *it's crowded*
ke ta thio   *both (and the two)*
yemato   *full*
alo   *other*

nosokomio   *hospital*
aftokinito   *car*
mera, meres   *day, days*
ikanopioimenos   *satisfied, happy*
moo aresi/then moo aresi   *I like/I don't like*
palio   *old (things)*
as elpisume   *let's hope*
then tha ehume   *we won't have*
provlima   *problem*
proto   *first,* theftero   *second,* telefteo   *last*
hartis, harti   *map*
venzinathiko   *petrol station*
skolio   *school*
(kane grigora!   *hurry up!*)
erhomaste   *we come/we're coming*
ipoyio   *underground*
kendrikos thromos   *main road (central road)*
fanaria   *lights (also used for traffic lights)*
hiliometro   *kilometre*
aftokinitothromos   *motorway*
venzini   *petrol*
posi, poses, posa   *how many*
litro   *litre*
mihani   *machine/engine*
zesti   *hot (adj.)*
saravalo   *'kaputt', wreck*

Kate Erhomaste apo ton ipoyio. O kendrikos thromos ine sta fanaria. Ine, isos tria hiliometra mehri ton aftokinitothromo. *(Ston aftokinitothromo)* Yati pai to aftokinito arga? Ehume arketi venzini? Posa litra? Ehume lathi? Ine i mihani poli zesti? Mas ethosan ena saravalo. Pu ine to kinito tilefono? Pu ine to numero too garaz? Pu ine i tsanda moo?

Tom Kate, se parakalo! Eho ponokefalo. Ke tora vrehi! Ke yati ine i astinomia piso mas?

kinito *mobile*	ponokefalo *headache*
garaz *garage (car mechanic's garage)*	vrohi *rain* (vrehi – *it's raining*)
tsanda *bag*	astinomia *police*

TOTAL NEW WORDS: 60
…only 31 words to go!

▶ Learn by heart

Someone has pranged the car and someone else is getting suspicious …! Try to say these lines fluently and like a prize-winning play!

Pame ya tenis

A Pame ya tenis. Moo aresun i thio Amerikani. Eho isitiria apo tin eteria moo. As parume to leoforio i kalitera pame me ton ipoyio. Ehi treno oli tin imera.

B Me to leoforio? Ton ipoyio? To treno? Yati? Ti simveni?* Ehume ena aftokinito eki kato.

A Eh … htes, me tin vrohi then itha ta fanaria. Ala ine mikro, mono i porta ke o mihanikos sto garaz itan poli kalos!

*Ti simeveni?: *What's the matter?*

Good news grammar

1 *moo, soo/sas, too, tis ... emena, esena, afton, aftin*

Learning these cold is difficult, but when they come up in the text or the **Flash cards** it's not so bad. Here's the first team:

moo	soo/sas	too	tis	mas	tus
my	*your*	*his*	*her*	*our*	*their*

The second team gives you some useful combinations. Spend five minutes learning them and take another five minutes to remember.

ya mena	ya sena	ya afton	ya aftin	ya mas	ya aftus
for me	*for you*	*for him*	*for her*	*for us*	*for them*

You use the same words with apo (*from*) and mazi me (*with*).

2 Last handful of verbs

Week 4 verbs – neatly lined up for easy learning. Ten minutes will do it.

I speak	milao	*I spoke*	milisa
I smoke	kapnizo	*I smoked*	kapnisa
I wait	perimeno	*I waited*	perimena
I like	moo aresi/moo aresun(e)	*I liked*	moo arese/aresan
I give	thino	*I gave*	ethosa

3 *Moo aresi/then moo aresi* (I like/I don't like)

You will use this all the time. Think how often you use *I like – I don't like* in English! Unfortunately it needs a bit of mental acrobatics, because in Greek *I like* is literally *it pleases me*: moo (*me*) aresi (*it pleases*).

If several things please you it's 'moo aresun'. Example: *I like the children* – moo aresun ta pethia. And if *you, he or she, we or they like* something it would be: **sas** aresi, **too** or **tis** aresi, **mas** aresi or **tus** aresi. So you have to rethink it quickly until it's as automatic as changing gear. Then: sas aresi o Tom Cruise? – Ne, ne!

4 last giftbox ... *erhome* (come)

Erhome is a rebel! Five minutes while you're grooming the dog.

	I	*you*	*he/she/it*	*we*	*they*
tora:	erhome	erhosaste	erhete	erhomaste	erhode
hthes:	iltha	ilthate	ilthe	ilthame	ilthan(e)

▶ Let's speak Greek

A ten-point warm-up: I give you an answer and you ask me a question as if you did not hear the words in CAPITAL LETTERS very well.

Example: O Nikos ine STO TAHITHROMIO. Pu ine o Nikos?

1 Ena tilefono ya TIN ELENI SOFIANU.
2 Emina sto nosokomio TON MARTIO.
3 O Tom theli na milisi ME TON KIRIO THIAMADI.
4 To isitirio me epistrofi ya tin Athina kostizi TRIANDA HILIATHES THRAHMES.
5 Then ehume kero ya ta FANARIA!
6 NE, ime ikanopioimenos me to spiti.
7 OHI, then lipame yati to fagito itan krio.
8 Pao stin Anglia ME TI FERRARI MOO.
9 Then ime ikanopioimenos me to spiti yati EHI POLA PROVLIMATA.
10 I thiakopes moo itan POLI KALES.

Answer in Greek using 'yes' or 'no'. Speak about yourself.

11 Ehis venzini?
12 Erhete to treno?
13 Pigenis ston stathmo?
14 Pigenis stin Larisa?
15 Kapnizis poli?

Explain these words in Greek. Your answers can vary from mine.

16 Daily help
17 Kennel
18 Teacher
19 Unemployed
20 To be broke

Answers

1 Ya pion ine to tilefono?
2 Pote emines sto nosokomio?
3 Se pion theli na milisi o Tom?
4 Poso kostizi to isitirio me epistrofi ya tin Athina?
5 Ya ti then ehume kero ya ta fanaria?
6 Ya ti ise ikanopioimenos me to spiti?
7 Yati then lipase pu to fagito itan krio?
8 Pos pas stin Anglia?
9 Yati then ise ikanopioimenos me to spiti?
10 Pos itan i thiakopes soo?
11 Ne, eho venzini.
12 Ohi, then erhete to treno.
13 Ohi, then pigeno ston stathmo.
14 Ne, pigeno stin Larisa.
15 Ohi, then kapnizo poli.
16 Voithia ya tin thulia sto spiti.
17 Mikro spiti ya skilous.
18 Kapios pu thulevi sto skolio.
19 Kapios pu then ehi thulia.
20 Otan then ehis lefta.

▶ Spot the keys

This time you plan a trip in the country and wonder about the weather.

You   Signomi, xerete ti kero kani avrio?

Answer   Lipame, then xero *ti kero kani* apo tin tileorasi *ala thiavasa stin efimeritha* oti o keros *tha ine astatos.* Apopse tha kani krio ke vrohi. *I thermocrasia* ine thekapende *vathmi* Kelsiou *ke tha ehi thinato anemo.*

He doesn't know something on television but you heard the word 'weather' and that it's going to be cold tonight and rainy. There's also something about 15 degrees Celsius, so you'd better take a jacket and an umbrella.

Test your progress

Translate in writing. Then check your answers and be amazed.

1 It is forbidden to go to the restaurant without shoes.
2 I like your Porsche. Was it very cheap?
3 When I am on holiday I always speak a lot of Greek.
4 I need six tickets. Do you have non-smoking seats?
5 I think that we have problems with the engine.
6 I do not like the Internet. It's difficult.
7 I do not understand. Can you speak more slowly, please?
8 It's hot and it's crowded. Let's go to the town.
9 One hour with her gives me a headache.
10 There is a bus at the traffic lights. Where's it going?
11 The credit card isn't here. We have to telephone the police.
12 Let's do it like this: first we buy the Ferrari for me and afterwards the T-shirt for you.
13 I like this car, but the other (one) was better.
14 We have only one litre of petrol and there isn't (hasn't) a petrol station until Athens.
15 I like the sun and I like the rain. I like both.
16 (*On the phone*) Hello, we're 20 km from Athens. Is (has) there any garage?
17 Excuse me. I need help, please. I do not know Athens. Where is the station?
18 The main road? It's not too difficult. You take the metro.
19 Where are they? What did they do? I do not like to wait.
20 We are coming from (the) platform 17? Where is Spiros?

06

week six

This is your last week! Need I say more?

Day one

- Read **At the airport**.
- Listen to/Read **Sto aerothromio**.
- Listen to/Read the **New words**. There are only a handful!

Day two

- Read **Sto aerothromio**. Learn all the **New words**.
- Work with the **Flash words** and **Flash sentences**.

Day three

- Test yourself on the **Flash sentences**.
- Listen to/Read **Learn by heart**.

Day four

- No more **Good news grammar!** Have a look at the summary.
- Read **Say it simply**.

Day five

- Listen to/Read **Let's speak Greek**.
- Listen to/Read **Spot the keys** (page 69).

Day six

- Your last **Test your progress**! Go for it!

Day seven

Congratulations!

You have successfully completed the course and can now speak

Instant Greek!

---

day-by-day guide

At the airport

Tom and Kate are on their way home to Birmingham. They are in the departure lounge at Athens airport.

Tom On Monday we must work. Terrible! I would prefer to go to Miami or Honolulu. Nobody knows where I am and the office can wait.

Kate And *my* company? What do they do? They speak with my mother! She has the number of our mobile. And then?

Tom Yes, yes, I know (it). Well, perhaps at Christmas we can go for a week in the snow or to Madeira on a ship ... There is a kiosk down there. I'll go and buy a newspaper ... Kate! There is Aristotelis Nikou!

Ari Hello, how are you? What are you doing here? This is my wife, Nancy. Are the holidays over? How were they?

Kate Greece is wonderful. We saw a lot and ate too much. We know Ahaia and Skiathos very well now.

Ari Next year Salonika! What a fantastic city! ... Mrs Walker, my wife would like to buy a book about computers. Can you go with her to help her, please. Mr Walker, you have a newspaper. Are there any photos of the football? And afterwards are we going to drink something?

(At the kiosk)

Kate There is nothing here. I do not see anything interesting. Are you also going to England?

Nancy No, we are going to Sparta to Aris' mother. Our children are often with her in the holidays. Tomorrow we'll take the train. It costs less.

Kate Your husband works at the Bank of Greece?

Nancy Yes. The work is interesting, but the money is little. We have an apartment, but it is small, and an old car. You always need a lot of work. My family lives in California and my girlfriend is in Florida and we write a lot of letters. I would like to go to America but it is too expensive.

⸺▶ Page 68

▶ Sto aerothromio

Tom and Kate are on their way home to Birmingham. They are
in the departure lounge at Athens airport.

Tom   Tin Theftera prepi na thulepsume. Apesio! Protimo na
pame sto Miami i stin Honolulu. Kanis then xeri pu ime ke
i eteria bori na perimeni.

Kate   Ke i eteria moo? Ti kanune? Milane stin mitera moo. Afti
ehi to numero too kinitu tilefonu mas. Ke tote?

Tom   Ne, ne, to xero. Lipon, isos ta Hristuyena borume na
pame ya mia evthomatha sto hioni i stin Madeira me
karavi ... Ine ena periptero eki kato. Pao na agoraso mia
efimeritha ... Kate! O Aristotelis Nikou!

Ari   Yasas, ti kanete? Ti kanete etho? Afti ine i yineka moo, i
Nancy. I thiakopes teliosan? Pos itan?

Kate   I Elatha ine iperohi. Ithame pola pragmata ke fagame para
poli. Xerume tin Ahaya ke tin Skiatho poli kala tora.

Ari   Tu hronu i Thesaloniki! Ti fandastiki poli! ... Kiria Walker, i
yineka moo theli na agorasi ena vivlio ya computer. Borite
na pate mazi tis na tin voithisete, parakalo? Kirie Walker,
ehete mia efimeritha. Ehi kamia fotografia pothosferu? Ke
meta pinume kati?

(Sto periptero)

Kate   Then ehi tipota etho. Then vlepo tipota enthiaferon. Pate
ke esis stin Anglia?

Nancy   Ohi, pame stin Sparti, stin mitera too Ari. Ta pethia mas
ine sihna mazi tis stis thiakopes. Avrio pernume to treno.
Kostizi pio ligo.

Kate   O anthras sas thulevi stin Trapeza tis Elathos?

Nancy   Ne. I thulia ehi enthiaferon ala ta lefta ine liga. Ehume ena
thiamerisma, ala ine mikro, ke ena palio aftokinito. Panda
hriazete poli thulia. I ikoyenia moo meni stin Kalifornia ke
i fili moo ine stin Floritha ke grafume pola gramata. Thelo
na pao stin Ameriki ala ine poli akriva.

┅━➤ Page 69

Kate   But you have a beautiful house in Porto Rafti.

Nancy   A house in Porto Rafti? I was never in Porto Rafti. When we have holidays we go to a friend in Pireus.

Tom   Kate, come quickly! We must go. Goodbye! What is the matter, Kate?

Kate   Wait, Tom, wait …!

▶ New words

aerothromio *airport*
protimo/protimisa *I prefer/ I preferred*
bori na perimeni *it can wait*
kanune *they do/make*
milane *they speak*
mitera *mother*
too *of*
ke tote? *and then?*
Hristuyena *Christmas*
hioni *snow*
karavi *boat*
eki kato *down there*
ti kanete? *How are you?*
teliosan *are finished*
iperohos/i/o *wonderful*
xerume *we know*
(tu) hronu *next year*

fandastikos/i/o *fantastic*
vivlio *book*
vlepo *I see*
sihna *often*
thiamerisma *apartment*
ikoyenia *family*
meni *he/she/it lives or stays;* meno/emina *I live/I lived*
grafume *we write;* grafo/egrapsa *I write/I wrote*
gramata *letters*
pote *never/ever*
otan *when*
ela! *come!*
ti simveni? *what's the matter?*
perimene/perimenete *wait! (familiar/formal)*

TOTAL NEW WORDS: 31
TOTAL GREEK WORDS LEARNED: 371
EXTRA WORDS: 81

GRAND TOTAL: 452

Kate	Ala ehete ena omorfo spiti sto Porto Rafti.
Nancy	Ena spiti sto Porto Rafti? Then imoon pote sto Porto Rafti. Otan ehume thiakopes pame se enan filo ston Pirea.
Tom	Kate, ela grigora! Prepi na pame. Adio! Ti simveni, Kate?
Kate	Perimene, Tom, perimene …!

▶ Learn by heart

This is your last dialogue to learn by heart. Give it your best!
You now have six prize-winning party pieces, and a large store
of everyday sayings which will be very useful.

Adio!

Kate	Parakalo. Kalimera kirie Thiamadi. Ime i Kate Walker. Imaste sto aerothromio. Ne, I thiakopes teliosan. I Elatha ine iperohi. O Tom theli na sas milisi. Mia stigmi parakalo, e … adio!
Tom	Ya, Pavlo! Ti? Agorases ke ta thio? Ine ena e-mail stin eteria moo? Iperoha! Efharisto poli! Too hronu? I Kate theli na pai stin Italia ala ego thelo na tho tin Thesaloniki. Me tin Edith Palmer? SE PARAKALO! Prepi na pame, lipon, tha se tho sindoma! Ya, adio!

▶ Spot the keys

Here is a final practice round. If you have the recording close the
book right NOW. This time the key words are not shown. When
you have found them see if you can get the gist of it. My answer
is on page 79.

This is what you might ask of a taxi driver:

Posa lepta mehri to aerothromio ke poso kostizi?

And this could be the reply:

Exartate pote pate. Kanonika perni ikosi lepta. Ala an ehi poli
kinisi ke ehi pola aftokinita stin yefira perni tulahiston
triandapende lepta. Borite na thiavasete tin timi sto tahimetro.
Ine metaxi theka hiliathes ke thekapende hiliathes thrahmes.

Good news grammar

As promised there is no new grammar in this section, just a summary of all the **Instant** verbs which appear in the six weeks. The second line of each entry is the past tense. The 30 verbs are not for learning, just for a quick check. You know and have used most of them!

	I	you	he/she/it	we	they
	ego	esis	aftos/afti/afto	emis	afti
be	ime	isaste	ine	imaste	ine
	imoon	*isaste*	*itan*	*imaste*	*itan(e)*
buy	agorazo	agorazete	agorazi	agorazume	agorazun(e)
	agorasa	*agorasate*	*agorase*	*agorasame*	*agorasan(e)*
can	boro	borite	bori	borume	borun(e)
	boresa	*boresate*	*borese*	*boresame*	*boresan(e)*
come	erhome	erhosaste	erhete	erhomaste	erhode
	iltha	*ilthate*	*ilthe*	*ilthame*	*ilthan(e)*
cost			costizi		costizun(e)
			costise		*costisan*
drink	pino	pinete	pini	pinume	pinun(e)
	ipia	*ipiate*	*ipie*	*ipiame*	*ipiane*
do	kano	kanete	kani	kanume	kanun(e)
	ekana	*kanate*	*ekane*	*kaname*	*ekanan*
eat	troo	trote	troi	trome	trone
	efaga	*fagate*	*efage*	*(e)fagame*	*fagane*
fix, repair	ftiahno	ftiahnete	ftiahni	ftiahnume	ftiahnun(e)
	eftiaxa	*ftiaxate*	*eftiaxe*	*ftiaxame*	*ftiaxan(e)*
give	thino	thinete	thini	thinume	thinun(e)
	ethosa	*thosate*	*ethose*	*thosame*	*thosane*
go	pao	pate	pai	pame	pane
	piga	*pigate*	*pige*	*pigame*	*pigan(e)*
have	eho	ehete	ehi	ehume	ehun(e)
	iha	*ihate*	*ihe*	*ihame*	*ihan(e)*
help	voitho	voithite	voithi	voithume	voithun(e)
	voithisa	*voithisate*	*voithises*	*voithisame*	*voithisan(e)*
know	xero	xerete	xeri	xerume	xerun(e)
	ixera	*xerate*	*ixere*	*xerame*	*xerane*
like			aresi		aresun(e)
			arese		*aresane*
live	meno	menete	meni	menume	menun(e)
	emina	*minate*	*emine*	*miname*	*minane*
must	prepi				
need	hriazome	hriazosaste	hriazete	hriazomaste	hriazode
	hriastika	*hriastikate*	*hriastike*	*hriastikame*	*hriastikan*

	I	you	he/she/it	we	they
prefer	protimo	protimite	protimi	protimume	protimun(e)
	protimisa	*protimisate*	*protimise*	*protimisame*	*protimisane*
say	leo	lete	lei	leme	lene
	ipa	*ipate*	*ipe*	*ipame*	*ipane*
see	vlepo	vlepete	vlepi	vlepume	vlepun(e)
	itha	*ithate*	*ithe*	*ithame*	*ithan(e)*
smoke	kapnizo	kapnizete	kapnizi	kapnizume	kapnizun(e)
	kapnisa	*kapnisate*	*kapnise*	*kapnisame*	*kapnisan*
speak	milao	milate	milai	milame	milane
	milisa	*milisate*	*milise*	*milisame*	*milisan(e)*
take	perno	pernete	perni	pernume	pernun(e)
	pira	*pirate*	*pire*	*pirame*	*pirane*
telephone	tilefono	tilefonite	tilefoni	tilefonume	tilefonun(e)
	tilefonisa	*tilefonisate*	*tilefonise*	*tilefonisame*	*tilefonisan*
think,	pistevo	pistevete	pistevi	pistevume	pistevun(e)
believe	*pistepsa*	*pistepsate*	*pistepse*	*pistepsame*	*pistepsan(e)*
wait	perimeno	perimenete	perimeni	perimenume	perimenun(e)
	perimena	*perimenate*	*perimene*	*perimename*	*perimenan*
want,	thelo	thelete	theli	thelume	thelun(e)
would like	*ithela*	*thelate*	*ithele*	*thelame*	*thelane*
work	thulevo	thulevete	thulevi	thulevume	thulevun(e)
	Thulepsa	*Thulepsate*	*Thulepse*	*Thulepsame*	*Thulepsan(e)*
write	grafo	grafete	grafi	grafume	grafun(e)
	egrapsa	*grapsate*	*egrapse*	*grapsame*	*grapsane*

Say it simply

1 Imagine you are at the dry cleaner's. You want to know if the item you have brought to be cleaned can be done by the end of the day since you are leaving for Athens early tomorrow morning. You also want to explain that the stain may be red wine.

Think of what you could say in simple Greek, using the words you know. Then write it down and compare it with my suggestion on page 78.

2 You are at the airport about to catch your flight home when you realize that you have left some clothes behind in the room of your hotel. You phone the hotel's housekeeper to ask her to send the things on to you.

What would you say? Formulate your telephone call and say it. Then write it down and compare it with my suggestion on page 78.

▶ Let's speak Greek

Here's a five-point warm-up. Answer these questions using the words in brackets.

1 Agorasate to thiamerisma? (ne)
2 Xerete ti kanune ta Hristuyena? (tipota)
3 Pote ithate ton anthra sas? (Htes)
4 Yati piyenete stin Anglia? (ikoyenia, meni, eki)
5 Pos ine i Elatha? (iperohi)

In your last exercise you are going to interpret again this time telling your Greek friend what others have said in English. Each time say the whole sentence OUT LOUD, translating the English words in brackets.

6 I fili moo ipe oti ... (the holidays are finished)
7 O John ipe oti ... (we are going to Venice next year)
8 I yineka moo theli na xeri ... (when you go to Los Angeles)
9 Episis theli na xeri ... (what they said)
10 O anthras moo lei oti ... (he cannot come)
11 I Angela then erhete yati ... (she works on a boat)
12 O filos moo lei oti ... (you are very nice)
13 Episis lei oti ... (he wants to have your phone number)
14 Ine kapios pu theli na xeri ... (what you did)
15 I mitera moo lei oti ... (she likes the shops)
16 Kanenas then xeri ... (where he has been in America)
17 I fili moo then xerun ... (who took the car)
18 Kapios xeri ... (how we can go to Salonika)
19 Then xero ... (how much it costs to fix)
20 I Kate Walker xeri ... (where you can buy **Instant Greek**)

Answers

1 Ne, to agorasa.
2 Then kanune tipota.
3 Ton itha htes.
4 I ikoyenia moo meni eki.
5 I Elatha ine iperohi.
6 i thiakopes teliosan.
7 pame stin Venetia tu hronu.
8 pote pate sto Los Angeles.
9 ti ipan.
10 then bori na elthi.

11 thulevi se ena karavi.
12 ise poli kalos.
13 theli to numero too tilefonu sas.
14 ti kanate.
15 tis aresun ta magazia.
16 pu pige stin Ameriki.
17 pios pire to aftokinito.
18 pos pame stin Thesaloniki.
19 poso kostizi na to ftiaxune.
20 pu borite na agorasete to **Instant Greek**.

Test your progress

Thirty **Instant** verbs have been crammed into this text! But don't panic – it looks worse than it is. Go for it – you'll do brilliantly!

Translate into Greek:

1 We write many letters because we have a new computer.
2 Hello, can I help? Your bag is not here? Where can it be?
3 Who knows the number of his mobile phone? I am sorry, I don't know it.
4 How are you? I am happy that you do not smoke.
5 Do you want to see Sparta? It's a big town.
6 I do not like January. There is snow and it is often very cold.
7 There is a kiosk down there. Would you like something to eat?
8 Why did they not phone? We waited until yesterday.
9 I took the book. He says it is interesting.
10 I believe that the airport is always open, day and night.
11 It is important to know (we) how much the client bought.
12 Have you seen the English newspaper? I do not like the photo. It is ugly.
13 He says that he has a cold. He thinks that he's coming tomorrow.
14 Is an apartment near the centre expensive in Greece?
15 We both have to work. Five children cost a lot.
16 I am going at Christmas. I have holidays in December and not (no) in July.
17 We know Pavlo very well. Do you like him?
18 Can you give me the dog? He is small but nice. What does he eat?
19 Her mother is here. She does not speak Greek. It is a little difficult for her.
20 Don't you know it? It costs 500,000 drs to fix (we).
21 I must go to the cash dispenser. I need money.
22 I am sorry but **Instant Greek** is finished (teliose).

answers

How to score

From a total of 100%:
- Subtract 1% for each wrong or missing word.
- Subtract 1% for the wrong form of the verb, like 'ime' when it should be 'imoon or imoona' or 'boro pame' instead of 'boro pao'.

There are no penalties for:
- Wrong endings of words, like 'kalos', when it should be 'kali'.
- Picking the wrong word where there are two of similar meaning.
- Wrong word order.
- Wrong spelling, as long as you can say the word! e.g. imuna/imoona'
- Missing out odd little words which might not be translated in English, like 'na, i, to, tis, ton', etc.

**100% LESS YOUR PENALTIES WILL GIVE
YOU YOUR WEEKLY SCORE**

For each test, correct your mistakes. Then read the corrected answers out loud twice.

Week 1 – Test your progress

1 Kalimera, imaste o Ari ke i Elke.
2 Ime apo tin Athina, ke esis?
3 Pu thulevete tora?
4 Imoona stin Athina ton Oktomvrio
5 I fili moo ine stin Elatha ya ena hrono.
6 Panda pame stin Rotho ton Iunio.
7 Thulepsa stin Fiat ton Maio.

8 Ti kanete sto Lonthino?
9 Thulevo se ena amerikaniko skolio.
10 To megalo spiti sto Porto Rafti ine ya ta pethia.
11 Mia stigmi parakalo, pu ine o Aristotelis?
12 Ehi to spiti tilefono? Thistihos ohi.
13 Kostizi mia Ferrari poli? Ne, vevea, kostizi para poli.
14 Pos ine i thulia stin Elatha, kali?
15 O Aristotelis ehi ena filo stin eteria moo.
16 Imaste stin Skiatho tris meres tora.
17 Ehume kales thesis sto aeroplano.
18 Panda eho varetes thiakopes.
19 Ehi mia omorfi yineka, ena Lamborghini ke pola lefta.
20 Isaste i kiria Onassis? Ehete ena megalo aeroplano.

YOUR SCORE: _____ %

Week 2 – Test your progress

1 Pu ine ena tilefono?
2 Signomi, ehume mono pistotiki karta.
3 Borume na pame stis epta avrio?
4 Ehete ena arketa megalo trapezi? Imaste pende.
5 Ta mikra thomatia then ehune banio.
6 Thelume na fame zabon ke psomakia.
7 Borume na pame apo tis exi mehri tis epta para tetarto.
8 Pu borume na piume kati etho konda?
9 Imaste sto bar apo tis enea mehri tis theka ke misi.
10 Entaxi, pernume to Rover ya mia mera.
11 Poso kostizi to proino? Mono thio hiliathes thrahmes.
12 Ti thelete? To computer? Then thulevi.
13 Pos ine i milopita. Kali ala akrivi.
14 Pu ine i tualetes, aristera i thexia?
15 Boro na pao sto Holliwood.
16 Ena kafe parakalo … pinume para poli kafe.
17 Pu ine i kiria Pavlithi? Isos sto bar?
18 Hilies thrahmes ya ena krio tsai? Ine ligo akrivo.
19 Imoona stin Rotho ton Fevruario. Then ine ashima.
20 Ine triakosia bar etho, ena ine trianda metra thexia.

YOUR SCORE: _____ %

Week 3 – Test your progress

1 Prota thelo na pao stin mihani analipsis.
2 Se afto to magazi ta paputsia kostizune para poli.
3 Ithate ton anthra moo sto farmakio?
4 Imaste etho mehri tis theka ke tetarto.
5 Ithame to tenis stin Anglia stin tileorasi.
6 Lipame ala then ehume to ithio se kokino, se numero
   saranda-tesera.
7 Afto to magazi then ine ftino.
8 Pios eftiaxe to tilefono moo? Esis?
9 Etho ine to polikatastima. Ala then ine anihto.
10 Simera then agorasame para pola pragmata. Mono psomi ke
   miso kilo vootiro.
11 Ta efaga ola – avga, mila, patates ke ena komati tiri.
12 Prepi na kanume ta psonia. Ine afto to kendro?
13 Hthes imoona stin eteria mehri tis enea.
14 I Anglikes efimerithes kostizun poli stin Elatha.
15 Ehi leoforio? Ohi? Then pirazi.
16 Itan enas poli kalos politis.
17 Ti ine afto? Kati ya mena?
18 Agorase tin tsanda etho konda i sto MINION?
19 Ola itane poli akriva. Etsi then agorasa tipota.
20 Hriazomaste tria kila, pistevo.

YOUR SCORE: _____ %

Week 4 – Test your progress

1 Kapios tilefonise ston kirio Thiamadi?
2 Thelo na xero pu ine to estiatorio.
3 Ine arga ke then ine eki. Ti kanume apopse?
4 Etho ine to menoo. Xerete ta krasia tis Ahaias?
5 I mihani analipsis ine epano, piso apo tin exotho, thipla stin porta.
6 Tin Tetarti prepi na pame ston yatro. Ine ena simandiko randevu.
7 Yati leo oti ine vareti? Yati tin xero kala.
8 Ton ithate? Prepi na pao stin Larisa mazi too.
9 O kirios Thiamadis ine pelatis moo.
10 Thelo na agoraso afto to pragma. Pos lene sta Elinika …?
11 Tin epomeni evthomatha? Lipame. Then ine thinaton.
12 Borite na me voithisete parakalo. Efharisto poli!
13 Ekato hiliathes thrahmes ya thio meres. Poli enthiaferon.
   Ne, fisika to pernume.

14 Prepi na agoraso tria pragmata ya tus filus moo.
15 Eho krio. Hriazome ena yatro.
16 Borune na fane mono ton baklava?
17 Ine enas apesios skilos. Ti borume na kanume?
18 Kanis then ithe pios efage tin brizola.
19 Boro na po kati: to kotopulo then ine ashimo, ala to psari ine kalitero.
20 Ti pernete? Ta fruta? Ne, vevea, ine apo tin Ahaia.

YOUR SCORE: _____ %

Week 5 – Test your progress

1 Apagorevete na pate sto estiatorio horis paputsia.
2 Moo aresi i Porsche sas. Itan poli ftini?
3 Otan ime se thiakopes milao Elinika poli.
4 Hriazome exi isitiria. Ehete mi-kapnizodes thesis?
5 Pistevo oti ehume provlimata me tin mihani.
6 Then moo aresi to Internet. Ine poli thiskolo.
7 Then katalaveno. Borite na milate pio arga parakalo?
8 Kani zesti ke ehi kosmo. Pame stin poli.
9 Mia ora mazi tis moo thini ponokefalo.
10 Sta fanaria ine ena leoforio. Pu pai?
11 I pistotiki karta then ine etho. Prepi na tilefonisume stin astinomia.
12 As to kanume etsi: prota agorazume ta Ferrari ya mena ke meta to bluzaki ya sena.
13 Moo aresi afto to aftokinito ala to alo itan kalitero.
14 Ehume mono ena litro venzini ke then ehi venzinathiko mehri tin Athina.
15 Moo aresi o ilios ke moo aresi i vrohi. Moo aresun ke ta thio.
16 Parakalo, imaste ikosi hiliometra apo tin Athina. Ehi kanena garaz?
17 Signomi. Hriazome voithia parakalo. Then xero tin Athina. Pu ine o stathmos?
18 O kendrikos thromos? Then ine poli thiskolo. An pernete ton ipoyio.
19 Pu itane? Ti ekanan? Then moo aresi na perimeno.
20 Erhomaste apo tin platforma theka-epta. Pu ine o Spiros?

YOUR SCORE: _____ %

Week 6 – Test your progress

1 Grafume pola gramata yati ehume ena computer.
2 Yasas, boro na voithiso? I tsanda sas then ine etho? Pu bori na ine?
3 Pios xeri to numero too kinitu tilefonu too? Lipame, then to xero.
4 Ti kanete? Ime ikanopioimenos pu then kapnizete alo.
5 Thelete na thite tin Sparti? Ine mia megali poli.
6 Then moo aresi o Ianuarios. Ehi hioni ke sihna kani krio.
7 Ine ena periptero eki kato. Thelete kati na fate?
8 Yati then tilefonisan? Perimename mehri htes.
9 Pira to vivlio. Lei oti ine poli enthiaferon.
10 Pistevo oti to aerothromio ine panda anihto, mera ke nihta.
11 Ine simandiko na xerume poso agorase o pelatis.
12 Ithes tin Angliki efimeritha? Then moo aresi i fotografia. Ine ashimi.
13 Lei oti ehi krio. Pistevi oti erhete avrio.
14 Ine ena thiamerisma konda sto kendro akrivo stin Elatha?
15 Ke i thio prepi na thulepsume. Pende pethia kostizun poli.
16 Piyeno ta Hristuyena. Eho tis thiakopes ton Thekemvrio ke ohi ton Iulio.
17 Xerume ton Pavlo poli kala. Sas aresi?
18 Borite na moo thosete ton skilo? Ine mikros ala kalos. Ti troi?
19 I mitera tis ine etho. Then milai Elinika. Ine ligo thiskolo ya aftin.
20 Then to xeris? Kostizi pendakosies hiliathes thrahmes na to ftiaxume.
21 Prepi na pao stin mihani analipsis. Hriazome lefta.
22 Lipame ala **Instant Greek** teliose.

YOUR SCORE: _____ %

Say it simply (Week 6)

1 Signomi, eho ena megalo provlima. Isos ine kokino krasi. Ala then ime veveos. Imaste sto xenothohio mehri avrio. Pame stin Athina stis epta. Borite na to kanete simera parakalo?

2 Parakalo. Kalimera, ime i Kate Walker. Tilefono apo to aerothromio. Imuna sto thomatio ikosithio ya tris meres. Lipame ala ine pragmata sto thomatio ke tora ime sto aerothromio ke pame sto Birmingham. Borite na me voithisete parakalo. To xenothohio xeri pu meno sto Birmingham. Efharisto poli.

Spot the keys (Week 6)

It depends when you are going. Normally it takes 20 minutes. But if there is a lot of traffic and a queue on the bridge, it takes at least 35 minutes. You can read the price on the meter. It will be between 10,000 and 15,000 drachmas.

how to use the flash cards

The **Flash cards** have been voted the best part of this course! Learning words and sentences can be tedious, but with flash cards it's quick and good fun.

This is what you do:

When the **Day-by-day guide** tells you to use the cards, cut them out. There are 18 **Flash words** and 10 **Flash sentences** for each week. Each card has a little number on it telling you to which week it belongs, so you won't cut out too many cards at a time or muddle them up later on.

First, try to learn the words and sentences by looking at both sides of the cards. Then, when you have a rough idea, start testing yourself. That's the fun bit. Look at the English, say the Greek, and then check. Make a pile for the 'correct' ones and one for the 'wrong' and 'don't know' ones. When all the cards are used up, start again with the 'wrong' pile and try to whittle it down until you get all of them right. You can also play it 'backwards' by starting with the Greek face-up.

Keep the cards in a little box or put an elastic band around them. Take them with you on the bus, the train, to the hairdresser's or the dentist's. If you find the paper too flimsy, photocopy the words and sentences onto card before cutting them up. You could also buy some plain card and stick them on or simply copy them out.

The 18 **Flash words** for each week are there to start you off. Convert the rest of the **New words** to **Flash words**, too. It's well worth it!

> ### FLASH CARDS for Instant LEARNING:
> ### DON'T LOSE THEM – USE THEM!

ehume _1_	ne _1_
parakal**o** _1_	**i**maste _1_
tr**a**peza _1_ ΤΡΑΠΕΖΑ	p**a**me _1_
p**a**o _1_	ap**o** _1_
imoona _1_	**i**ne _1_
pol**i** _1_	**o**morfos _1_

yes [1]	we have [1]
we are, we were [1]	please [1]
we/let's go [1]	bank [1]
from [1]	I go, I'm going [1]
he/she/it is [1]	I was [1]
beautiful [1]	very, much, a lot [1]

ti **1**	pu **1**
eho **1**	**t**ora **1**
kalisp**e**ra **1**	kal**o**s/kal**i**/ kal**o** **1**
l**i**go **2**	eth**o** **2**
arister**a** **2**	arket**a** **2**
al**a** **2**	p**o**so kost**i**zi? **2**

where [1]	what [1]
now [1]	I have [1]
good, nice [1]	good evening [1]
here [2]	little [2]
enough [2]	left [2]
how much? [2]	but [2]

ohi 2	proin**o** 2
ent**a**xi 2	**a**vrio 2
k**a**ti 2	m**o**no 2
thexi**a** 2	ke 2
isia 2	ts**a**i 2
logariasm**o**s 2	akriv**o** 2

breakfast	2	no	2
tomorrow	2	OK	2
only	2	something	2
and	2	right	2
tea	2	straight on	2
expensive	2	bill	2

3 si**me**ra	**3** pr**e**pi
3 lip**a**me	**3** leofori**o**
3 tahithrom**io** ΤΑΧΥΔΡΟΜΕΙΟ	**3** **o**lo
3 met**a**	**3** th**e**lo
3 magaz**i**	**3** m**e**hri
3 p**o**te	**3** arg**o**tera

must **3**	today **3**
bus **3**	I'm sorry **3**
all **3**	post office **3**
I want **3**	after, afterwards **3**
until **3**	shop **3**
later **3**	when **3**

3 eth**o**	**3** kom**a**ti
3 hthes	**3** kond**a**
3 pi**o**s	**3** aft**o**
4 k**a**pios	**4** yat**i**
4 x**e**ro	**4** randev**u**
4 simandik**o**	**4** efharist**o** pol**i**

3 piece	**3** here
3 near	**3** yesterday
3 this	**3** who
4 why/ because	**4** someone
4 appointment	**4** I know
4 many thanks	**4** important

4 thinat**os**	**4** enthiaf**e**ron
4 estiat**o**rio	**4** ap**e**sio
4 **a**rostos/ **a**rosti	**4** yatr**os**
4 ps**a**ri	**4** bor**o**
4 kr**e**as	**4** sal**a**ta
4 ner**o**	**4** kan**is**

4 interesting	**4** possible
4 terrible	**4** restaurant
4 doctor	**4** sick
4 I can	**4** fish
4 salad	**4** meat
4 nobody/ anybody	**4** water

aftokinito [5]	nosokomio [5] ΝΟΣΟΚΟΜΕΙΟ
apagorevete [5]	grigora! [5]
gramato- kivotio [5]	isitirio [5]
ke ta thio [5]	kendrikos [5] thromos
mera, meres [5]	mi- kapnizodes [5]
moo aresi [5]	then moo [5] aresi

5 hospital	**5** car
5 quickly!	**5** it's forbidden
5 ticket	**5** letter-box
5 main road	**5** both (and the two)
5 non-smoking	**5** day, days
5 I don't like	**5** I like

5 pi**o**	5 st**a**si ΣΤΑΣΗ
5 stathm**os** ΣΤΑΘΜΟΣ	5 tr**e**no
5 venzin**a**thiko ΒΕΝΖΙΝΑΔΙΚΟ	5 yem**a**to
6 aerothr**o**mio ΑΕΡΟΔΡΟΜΙΟ	6 mit**e**ra
6 Hrist**u**yena	6 hi**o**ni
6 kar**a**vi	6 per**i**ptero

bus stop **5**	more **5**
train **5**	railway station **5**
full **5**	petrol station **5**
mother **6**	airport **6**
snow **6**	Christmas **6**
kiosk **6**	boat **6**

6 iperohos	6 xerume
6 fandastikos	6 vivlio
6 sihna	6 thiamerisma
6 ikoyenia	6 meno/emina
6 grafo/ egrapsa	6 gramata
6 pote	6 perimenete!

6 we know	**6** wonderful
6 book	**6** fantastic
6 apartment	**6** often
6 I live/I lived	**6** family
6 letters	**6** I write/ I wrote
6 wait!	**6** never/ever

Kalimera, ime o/i … 1

Mia stigmi, parakalo 1

Pame stin Kerkika 1

I Patra ine poli omorfi 1

Thulevo sto Lonthino 1

ya tin eteria moo 1

Pu thulevete? 1

Imaste se thiakopes tora 1

Ehume ena spiti 1

Imaste stin Elatha
ton Avgusto 1

Good morning, I am … [1]

a moment, please [1]

We are going to Corfu [1]

Patras is very beautiful [1]

I work in London [1]

for my company [1]

Where do you work? [1]

We are on holiday now [1]

We have a house. [1]

We were in Greece
in August [1]

Ehete thom**a**tio? 2

Pu **i**ne to thom**a**tio? 2

Poso kost**i**zi? 2

Ti **o**ra? 2

Th**e**lume na p**a**me stin Ath**i**na 2

Stis okt**o** ke mis**i** 2

Ine pol**i** akriv**o** 2

Ip**a**rhi **e**na bar eth**o?** 2

K**a**ti na f**a**me 2

Ton logariasm**o**, parakal**o** 2

Do you have a room? **2**

Where is the room? **2**

How much does it cost? **2**

At what time? **2**

We want (would like) to **2**
go to Athens

At half past eight **2**

It is too expensive **2**

Is there a bar here? **2**

Something to eat **2**

The bill, please **2**

Pistevo **oti** ... 3

Prepi na pame 3

Thelo na pao ya psonia 3

Prepi na pao stin trapeza 3

Mehri pote? 3

Iparhi ena magazi? 3

Then pirazi 3

Agorasa pola pragmata 3

Ine poli kalos 3

Konda sto tahithromio 3

I believe that … **3**

We must go **3**

I want to go shopping **3**

I must go to the bank **3**

Until when? **3**

Is there a shop? **3**

It doesn't matter **3**

I have bought too much **3**

He is very nice **3**

Near the post office **3**

Iparhi kapios

4

Then ipe

4

Tin epomeni evthomatha

4

Brosta stin porta

4

Piso apo tin eklisia

4

Then ehume ora

4

Pame na fame

4

Pao mazi too

4

Voithia, parakalo

4

Pos lene sta Elinika …?

4

Is there someone? 4

He did not say 4

Next week 4

In front of the door 4

Behind the church 4

We don't have time 4

We are going to eat 4

I('ll) go with him 4

Help, please 4

How do you say 4
in Greek …?

me epistrofi ⁵

Lipame, then katalaveno ⁵

Borite na milisete ⁵
pio arga?

Ti ora ehi treno? ⁵

Ime poli ikanopioimenos ⁵

Moo aresi to Rover ⁵

Moo aresi yati ine ⁵
kenuryio

Moo aresune ke ta thio ⁵

Then moo aresi to krasi ⁵

Borume na kapnisume ⁵
etho?

return (ticket) 5

I am sorry,
I don't understand 5

Can you speak more
slowly? 5

At what time is there
a train? 5

I am very satisfied 5

I like the Rover 5

I like it because it is new 5

I like both 5

I don't like the wine 5

Can we smoke here? 5

Kanis then to xeri

6

Then to xero

6

Ti simveni?

6

Ti ipe?

6

Ti kanune?

6

Ti kanete?

6

Then vlepo …

6

Then ine tipota

6

I ikoyenia moo meni stin Anglia

6

Pame se ena filo

6

Nobody knows it **6**

I don't know it **6**

What is the matter? **6**

What did he say? **6**

What are they doing? **6**

How are you? **6**

I don't see … **6**

There is nothing **6**

My family lives in England **6**

We are going to
a friend's **6**

InstantGreek InstantGreek InstantGreek InstantGreek

*This is to certify
that*

....

*has successfully completed
a six-week course of*

Instant Greek

with .... results

Elizabeth Smith

Date   *Instructor*